Living Language™

CONVERSATIONAL FRENCH

Living Spanish
Living French
Living Italian
Living German
Living Japanese
Living Russian
Living Portuguese (South American)
Living Portuguese (Continental)
Living Hebrew
Living Swahili
Children's Living French
Children's Living Spanish
Advanced Living French
Advanced Living Spanish
Living English for Spanish-Speaking People
Living English for French-Speaking People
Living English for Italian-Speaking People
Living English for German-Speaking People
Living English for Portuguese-Speaking People
Living English for Chinese-Speaking People
Living Language™ Spanish Video
Living Language™ French Video

Living Language™

CONVERSATIONAL FRENCH

A COMPLETE COURSE IN EVERYDAY FRENCH

By Ralph Weiman

EDUCATIONAL DIRECTOR LIVING LANGUAGE COURSES. FORMERLY CHIEF OF LANGUAGE SECTION, U.S. WAR DEPARTMENT

SPECIALLY PREPARED FOR USE WITH THE LIVING LANGUAGE COURSE IN FRENCH

Crown Publishers, Inc., New York

This work was previously published under the title *Conversation Manual French*.

THE LIVING LANGUAGE COURSE is a registered trademark and LIVING LANGUAGE is a trademark of Crown Publishers, Inc., One Park Avenue, New York, New York 10016

Manufactured in the United States of America.

Library of Congress Catalog Card Number: 55-12163

ISBN 0-517-55784-3

1985 Updated Edition

TABLE OF CONTENTS

INTRODUCTION to the COMPLETE LIVING LANGUAGE COURSE®

The Living Language Course® uses the natural method of language-learning. You learn French the way you learned English—by hearing the language and repeating what you heard. You didn't begin by studying grammar; you first learned how to say things, how words are arranged, and only when you knew the language pretty well did you begin to study grammar. This course teaches you French in the same way. Hear it, say it, absorb it through use and repetition. The only difference is that in this course the basic elements of the language have been carefully selected and condensed into 40 short lessons. When you have finished these lessons, you will have a good working knowledge of the language. If you apply yourself, you can master this course and learn to speak basic French in a few weeks.

While *Living Language™ Conversational French* is designed for use with the complete Living Language Course®, this book may be used without the cassettes. The first 5 lessons cover French pronunciation, laying the foundation for learning the vocabulary, phrases, and grammar that are explained in the later chapters.

All the material is presented in order of importance. When you reach page 150, you will have already learned 300 of the most frequently used sentences and will be able to make yourself understood on many important topics. By the time you have finished this course, you will have a sufficient command of French to get along in all ordinary situations.

The brief but complete summary of French grammar is included in the back of this book to enable you to perfect your knowledge of French. There are also many other helpful features, such as vocabulary tips, practice exercises, and verb charts. The special section on letter-writing will show you how to answer an invitation, make a business inquiry, and address an envelope properly. Just as important is the *Living Language™ Common Usage Dictionary.* This is included in the course primarily for use as a reference book, but it is a good idea to do as much browsing in it as possible. It contains the most common French words with their meanings illustrated by everyday sentences and idiomatic expressions. The basic words—those you should learn from the start—are capitalized to make them easy to find.

Keep practicing your French as much as possible. Once you are well along in the course, try reading French magazines, newspapers, and books. Use your French whenever you get a chance—with French-speaking friends, with the waiter at a French restaurant, with other students.

This course tries to make the learning of French as easy and enjoyable as possible, but a certain amount of application is necessary. The cassettes and books that make up this course provide you with all the material you need; the instructions on the next page tell you what to do. The rest is up to you.

Course Material

The material of the complete Living Language Course® consists of the following:

1. *2 hour-long cassettes.* The label on each face indicates clearly which lessons are contained on that side. (Living French is also available on 4 long-playing records.)

2. *Conversational French book.* This book is designed for use with the recorded lessons, or it may be used alone. It contains the following sections:

    Basic French Vocabulary and Grammar
    Summary of French Grammar
    Verb Charts
    Letter-writing

3. *French-English/English-French Common Usage Dictionary.* A special kind of dictionary that gives you the literal translations of more than 20,000 French words, plus idiomatic phrases and sentences illustrating the everyday use of the more important vocabulary and 1,000 essential words capitalized for ready reference.

How to Use Conversational French with the Living Language™ Cassettes

TO BEGIN

There are 2 cassettes with 10 lessons per side. The beginning of each lesson is announced on the tape and each lesson takes approximately 3 minutes. If your cassette player has a digit indicator, you can locate any desired point precisely.

LEARNING THE LESSONS

1. Look at page 1. Note the words in **boldface** type. These are the words you will hear on the cassette. There are pauses to enable you to repeat each word and phrase right after you hear it.

2. Now read Lesson 1. (The symbols indicate the beginning of the recorded material. In some advanced lessons, information and instructions precede the recording.) Note the points to listen for when you play the cassette. Look at the first word: **Albert**, and be prepared to follow the voice you will hear.

3. Play the cassette, listen carefully, and watch for the points mentioned. Then rewind, play the lesson again, and this time say the words aloud. Keep repeating until you are sure you know the lesson. The more times you listen and repeat, the longer you will remember the material.

4. Now go on to the next lesson. It's always good to quickly review the previous lesson before starting a new one.

5. There are 2 kinds of quizzes at the end of each section. One is the matching type, in which you must select the English translation of the French sentence. In the other, you fill in the blanks with the correct French word chosen from the 3 given directly below the sentence. Do these quizzes faithfully and, if you make any mistakes, reread the section.

6. When you get 100 percent on the Final Quiz, you may consider that you have mastered the course.

Living Language™

CONVERSATIONAL FRENCH

LESSON 1

1. THE LETTERS AND SOUNDS

(Letters and Sounds I)

A. Most French sounds are like English. Listen to and repeat the following French names and notice which sounds are similar and which are different: [1]

Albert	**Jacques**	**Paul**
André	**Jean**	**Paulette**
Charles	**Jeanne**	**René**
Claire	**Jérôme**	**Richard**
Denise	**Jules**	**Robert**
François	**Louis**	**Roger**
Françoise	**Lucie**	**Simone**
Georges	**Marie-Louise**	**Suzanne**
Hélène	**Marie-Rose**	**Yvette**
Henri	**Marie-Thérèse**	**Yvonne**

NOTICE:

1. that each sound is pronounced clearly and crisply—that sounds are not slurred over the way they often are in English.
2. that each syllable is spoken evenly, with a slight stress on the last one.

[1] The voices on the tapes were chosen to give you a selection of French accents. You will note that the first man's voice pronounces the final, normally mute *-e* in such words as *Clair-e, Denise-e*. This is a regionalism from the South of France, and it is also heard in the classical theatre when the works of such playwrights as Racine and Corneille are performed. The woman and the second man who are introduced later in the course speak in standard French and omit the sound of the final *-e*.

3. that the cedilla (¸) is placed under the letter *c (ç)* to show that it has the sound of *s* before *a, o* and *u:*

François *Frank*

4. that there are three marks (called "accents") used over French vowels:

   a. acute accent (´) placed over the letter *e:*

   André

   b. grave accent (`) placed over *a, e, u:*

   Hélène

   c. circumflex accent (ˆ) placed on *a, e, i, o, u:*

   Jérôme

These accents usually indicate the pronunciation of the vowel but in a few cases they distinguish words:

ou	or	*où*	where
la	the	*là*	there

B. Now listen to and repeat the following words which are similar in English and French. Notice how French spelling and pronunciation differ from English:

adresse	address
âge	age
ambitieux	ambitious
américain	American
banque	bank
bref	brief
bureau	desk; office
café	coffee; café
chef	chief

chèque	check
cinéma	cinema, movies
civilisation	civilization
condition	condition
curieux	curious
démocratie	democracy
différence	difference
difficulté	difficulty
excellent	excellent
garage	garage
grand	big, grand
guide	guide
hôtel	hotel
impartial	impartial
important	important
journal	journal, newspaper
lettre	letter

LESSON 2

(Letters and Sounds II)

ligne	line
machine	machine
nation	nation
nécessaire	necessary
opéra	opera
ordinaire	ordinary
papier	paper
possible	possible
potentiel	potential
principal	principal

problème	problem
public	public
question	question
radio	radio
restaurant	restaurant
sérieux	serious
signal	signal
silence	silence
station	station
suggestion	suggestion
télégramme	telegram
téléphone	telephone
thé	tea
théâtre	theatre
train	train
visite	visit

NOTES

1. Final consonants are not pronounced except for *c, r, f* and *l* (the consonants in CaReFuL):

NOT PRONOUNCED

moment	moment	**Richard**	Richard
sérieux	serious	**Jacques**	Jack

PRONOUNCED

public	public	**chef**	chief
cher	dear	**hôtel**	hotel

2. *e* is silent at the end of words of more than one syllable:

télégraphe	telegraph	**adresse**	address
	histoire	history	

3. *h* is never pronounced:

Henri	Henry	**hôtel**	hotel

4. *ch* is pronounced like the English *sh:*

chef	chief	**machine**	machine

5. *j.* is pronounced like the *s* in *pleasure, measure:*

Jean	John	**journal**	newspaper

6. *g* is like the *g* in *go* before *a, o* and *u:*

		garage	garage

—is like the *s* in *pleasure* (or French j) before *e* or *i:*

général	general	**Georges**	George
		danger	danger

7. *c* is pronounced like *k* before *a, o* and *u:*

café	coffee; café	**condition**	condition
		curieux	curious

—like *s* before *e* or *i:*

certain	certain	**cinéma**	movies
		police	police

8. *gu* is like the *g* in *go:*

		guide	guide

9. *qu* is pronounced *k:*

		question	question

10. *gn* is pronounced like the *ni* in *onion* or the *ny* in *canyon:*

signe	sign	**signal**	signal

11. *s* between vowels is like English z:

civilisation	civilization	**visite**	visit

12. *ss* between vowels is like English *s* in *see:*

possible	possible	**nécessaire**	necessary

13. *t* is like the English *t* except in the following combinations where it is like *s* in *see: -tion, -tial, -tiel, -tieux* (that is, before *i).*

-tion is pronounced like English *see-on:*

station	station	**condition**	condition
	nation	nation	

-tie is like English *see:*

démocratie democracy

-tial is like *see-al:*

impartial impartial

-tiel is like see-el:

potentiel potential

-tieux is like *see-uh:*

ambitieux ambitious

-stion is like English stee-on:

question question
suggestion suggestion

LESSON 3

2. PRONUNCIATION PRACTICE

(Pronunciation Practice I)

The following groups of words will give you some additional practice in spelling and pronounciation:

1. The sound *a* in *ah* or *father:*

madame	madam, Mrs.	**table**	table
date	date	**page**	page

2. The sound *ee* in *see* or *i* in *police* but cut off sharply (that is, not drawled):

ami	friend	**il**	he
ici	here	**facile**	easy
vie	life	**difficile**	difficult

3. The sound *o* as in *go* but not drawled:

hôtel	hotel	**au**	to the
chose	thing	**aussi**	also
mot	word	**eau**	water
	beau	beautiful, pretty	

Notice the various French spellings for this sound: *o, au, eau.*

4. The sound *e* in *get* but not drawled:

elle	she	**scène**	scene
il est	he is	**père**	father
très	very	**j'ai**	I have
	raison	reason	

Notice the various French spellings for this sound: *e, è, ai.*

5. The sound *ay* in *day* but not drawled:

café	coffee; café	**cinéma**	cinema, movies
téléphone	telephone	**donner**	to give
	Donnez!	Give!	

Notice the various spellings for this sound: *é*, the ending *-er* in words of more than one syllable and the ending *-ez*.

6. The sound *o* in *north* but shorter and more rounded:

note	note	**force**	force
homme	man	**ordre**	order
	Donnez!	Give!	

7. The sound *ou* as in *group* but not drawled:

ou	or	**jour**	day
où	where	**pour**	for
nous	we	**toujours**	always

8. The sound *u* in *burn*:

le	the	**cela**	that
de	of	**ceci**	this
je	I	**petit**	small

9. The sound spelled *u* in French. There is no similar sound in English. To make it, round the lips as though to pronounce *o* in *go* and without moving them say *ee* (that is, it is an *ee* sound pronounced with the lips rounded and slightly protruded). Listen carefully:

tu	you (familiar)	**plume**	pen
du	of the	**minute**	minute
rue	street	**utile**	useful
vue	view, sight	**su**	known
	lu	read	

LESSON 4

(Pronunciation Practice II)

10. The sound spelled *eu*. The nearest sound in English is the vowel in *burn*. You can make the French sound by saying the *u* in *burn* with your lips rounded and slightly protruded. Listen carefully:

peu	a little	**jeune**	young
deux	two	**leur**	their
peuple	people	**auteur**	author
neuf	nine	**mieux**	better
	soeur	sister	

Notice that this sound is spelled two ways: *eu* and *oeu*.

11. The sound *wah* (spelled *oi* in French):

moi	me	**voici**	here is, there are
trois	three	**voilà**	there is, there are
trois fois	three times	**avoir**	to have
	histoire	story	

12. The sound spelled *ui*:

lui	to him, her	**je suis**	I am
huit	eight	**aujourd'hui**	today

13. *ou* before a vowel sounds like the *w* in *west:*

oui	yes	**Louis**	Louis
ouest	west	**Edouard**	Edward

14. The nasal vowels. Certain vowels when followed by *n* (in a few cases *m)* are pronounced through the nose. Listen to the following examples:

a. Words with *an, en, am, em*:

an	year	**en**	in
dans	in	**enveloppe**	envelope
grand	big, large	**accent**	accent
France	France	**temps**	time

b. Words with *in, im, ain, aim, ien, oin*:

chemin	road	**américain**	American
simple	simple	**faim**	hunger
important	important	**bien**	well
train	train	**combien**	how much
	coin	corner	

c. Words with *on, om*:

bon	good	**savon**	soap
mon	my	**long**	long
garçon	boy, waiter	**bombe**	bomb

d. Words with *un, um*:

un	one	**quelqu'un**	somebody
lundi	Monday	**humble**	humble

LESSON 5

(Pronounciation Practice III)

15. The sound *y* in *yes* (spelled *y, -i-, -ail-, -eil-, -eill-, -ill-*, etc.):

les yeux	the eyes	**soleil**	sun
voyage	voyage	**meilleur**	better
papier	paper	**billet**	ticket
mieux	better	**fille**	daughter
travail	work	**famille**	family

16. The sound *sh* (spelled *ch* in French):

cher	dear	**chose**	thing
chercher	to look for	**riche**	rich

17. The sound of *s* in *pleasure*:

joli	pretty	**âge**	age
jour	day	**rouge**	red
déjà	already	**origine**	origin

Notice that this sound is spelled with both *j* and *g* (*g* only before *e* and *i*).

18. The *ni* in *onion* or the *ny* in canyon (spelled *gn* in French):

ligne	line	**Espagne**	Spain
signe	sign	**signal**	signal
	espagnol	Spanish	

19. Notice that the *r* sounds something like a gargle:

rouge	red	**par**	by
frère	brother	**parler**	to speak

Notice that the final *r* is pronounced in words of one syllable but not in words of more than one syllable (there are a few exceptions which will be treated later):

	par	by
But—		
	parler	to speak
	mer	sea
But—		
	aimer	to love

20. Notice the pronunciation of *-re* at the end of a word:

lettre	letter	**livre**	book
nombre	number	**quatre**	four

21. Notice the pronunciation *-le* at the end of a word:

table	table	**simple**	simple
	peuple	people	

3. THE FRENCH ALPHABET

Letter	*Name*	*Letter*	*Name*	*Letter*	*Name*
a	a	**j**	ji	**s**	esse
b	bé	**k**	ka	**t**	té
c	cé	**l**	elle	**u**	u
d	dé	**m**	emme	**v**	vé
e	e	**n**	enne	**w**	double vé
f	effe	**o**	o		
g	gé	**p**	pé	**x**	iks
h	ache	**q**	ku	**y**	i grec
i	i	**r**	erre	**z**	zède

LESSON 6

4. BUILDING UP A VOCABULARY

Building up a French vocabulary is a rather easy matter since a great number of words are similar in French and English. Many words are spelled exactly the same (though they may differ considerably in pronunciation):

art	art	*police*	police
date	date	*cause*	cause
exact	exact	*effort*	effort
place	place	*force*	force
message	message	*second*	second
passage	passage	*excuse*	excuse
village	village	*source*	source
central	central	*capable*	capable
original	original	*probable*	probable
chance	chance	*possible*	possible
distance	distance	*terrible*	terrible
intelli-gence	intelli-gence	*visible*	visible
		double	double

patience	patience	*action*	action
science	science	*conversa-*	conversa-
certain	certain	*tion*	tion
point	point	*descrip-*	descrip-
direct	direct	*tion*	tion
respect	respect	*direction*	direction
article	article	*exception*	exception
automo-	automo-	*instruction*	instruction
bile	bile	*intention*	intention
fruit	fruit	*satisafac-*	satisfac-
justice	justice	*tion*	tion
	situation	situation	

There are many words spelled exactly the same except that the French word has an accent:

éducation	education	*récent*	recent
général	general	*différence*	difference
spécial	special	*expérience*	experience
grâce	grace	*extrême*	extreme
préface	preface	*privilège*	privilege
élément	element	*sincère*	sincere
évident	evident	*région*	region
présent	present	*émotion*	emotion
président	president	*révolution*	revolution
	zéro	zero	

In many cases the word is similar except that the French word ends in *-e:*

acte	act	*méthode*	method
affaire	affair	*moderne*	modern
aide	aid	*origine*	origin
blonde	blond	*poste*	post
capitale	capital	*rapide*	rapid
charme	charm	*riche*	rich
classe	class	*sorte*	sort

forme	form	*soupe*	soup
groupe	group	*terme*	term
liste	list	*verbe*	verb

In some cases there are other slight differences:

adresse	address	*cercle*	circle
immédiat	immediate	*problème*	problem
lac	lake	*matériel*	material
parc	park	*ouest*	west
rasoir	razor	*appétit*	appetite
sens	sense	*chapitre*	chapter
agréable	agreeable	*médecine*	medicine
confort-	comfort-	*signe*	sign
able	able	*ligne*	line
désagré-	disagree-	*coton*	cotton
able	able	*façon*	fashion
remarqu-	remark-	*nord*	north
able	able	*oncle*	uncle
langage	language	*raison*	reason
mariage	marriage	*saison*	season
	système	system	

idée	idea	*personne*	person
rivière	river	*commun*	common
circon-	circum-	*numéro*	number
stance	stance	*sud*	south
exemple	example	*peuple*	people
développe-	develop-		
ment	ment		

gouverne-	govern-	*diction-*	diction-
ment	ment	*naire*	ary
capitaine	captain	*manière*	manner
complet	complete	*membre*	member
crème	cream	*nombre*	number
enveloppe	envelope	*ordre*	order
	est	east	

GENERAL EQUIVALENTS

1. French *-é* = English *-y:*

beauté	beauty	*quantité*	quantity
nécessité	necessity	*réalité*	reality
qualité	quality	*société*	society
	université	university	

2. French *-ie* = English *-y:*

comédie	comedy	*industrie*	industry
copie	copy	*philoso-phie*	philosophy

3. French *-tie* = English *-cy:*

démocratie	democracy	*diplomatie*	diplomacy

4. French *-nce* = English *-ncy:*

tendance tendency

5. French *-eur* = English *-or* (*-er*):

acteur	actor	*faveur*	favor
conducteur	conductor	*inférieur*	inferior
directeur	director	*moteur*	motor
docteur	doctor	*porteur*	porter
erreur	error	*supérieur*	superior
	visiteur	visitor	

6. French *-oire* = English *-ory:*

gloire	glory	*mémoire*	momory
histoire	history	*territoire*	territory
	victoire	victory	

7. French *-ique* = English *ic*(*al*):

comique	comic(al)	*musique*	musical
critique	critic	*politique*	political
logique	logical	*pratique*	practical

8. French *-ment* = English *-ly:*

absolument	absolutely	*certainement*	certainly
	naturellement	naturally	

9. French *-aire* = English *-ary:*

anniversaire	anniversary	*militaire*	military
contraire	contrary	*secrétaire*	secretary

10. French *-é* = English *-ed:*

arrangé	arranged	*découragé*	discouraged
	sacré	sacred	

11. French *-ès* = English *-ess:*

progrès	progress	*succès*	success

12. French *-eux* = English *-ous:*

curieux	curious	*fameux*	famous
dangereux	dangerous	*merveilleux*	marvelous
	précieux	precious	

13. French *-iste* = English-*ist:*

artiste	artist	*journaliste*	journalist
dentiste	dentist	*pianiste*	pianist

14. French *-et* = English *-ect:*

effet	effect	*projet*	project
objet	object	*sujet*	subject

15. French (ˆ) = English *s:*

côté	coast	*hôpital*	hospital
coûter	to cost	*hôte*	host
fête	feast	*intérêt*	interest
forêt	forest	*maître*	master

16. French *é-* = English initial *s-:*

école	school	*étudiant*	student
étrange	strange	*étudier*	to study

17. French *es-* = English initial *s-:*

espace	space	*espagnol*	*Spanish*
Espagne	Spain	*esprit*	spirit
	estomac	stomach	

5. USEFUL WORD GROUPS

(Useful Word Groups I)

THE DAYS OF THE WEEK

lundi[1]	Monday
mardi	Tuesday
mercredi	Wednesday
jeudi	Thursday
vendredi	Friday
samedi	Saturday
dimanche	Sunday

THE MONTHS

janvier	January
février	February
mars	March
avril	April
mai	May
juin	June

[1] Notice that when you give the days of the week in French you begin with Monday. Notice also that the days of the week and the names of the months are not capitalized.

juillet	July
août	August
septembre	September
octobre	October
novembre	November
décembre	December

SOME NUMBERS

un	one
deux	two
trois	three
quatre	four
cinq	five
six	six
sept	seven
huit	eight
neuf	nine
dix	ten

SOME COLORS

bleu	blue
rouge	red
jaune	yellow
vert	green
blanc	white
noir	black
brun	brown
marron	chestnut color
gris	gray

NORTH, SOUTH, EAST, WEST

nord	North
sud	South
est	East
ouest	West

QUIZ 1

Try matching the following two columns:

1. *dimanche*	1. Thursday
2. *août*	2. chestnut color
3. *mercredi*	3. ten
4. *gris*	4. Sunday
5. *jeudi*	5. red
6. *neuf*	6. August
7. *marron*	7. Monday
8. *huit*	8. July
9. *juillet*	9. five
10. *jaune*	10. white
11. *rouge*	11. grey
12. *lundi*	12. nine
13. *cinq*	13. Wednesday
14. *blanc*	14. yellow
15. *dix*	15. eight

ANSWERS

1—4; 2—6; 3—13; 4—11; 5—1; 6—12; 7—2; 8—15; 9—8; 10—14; 11—5; 12—7; 13—9; 14—10; 15—3.

WORD STUDY

The Word Studies point out words which are similar in French and English.

le charme	charm
la classe	class
considérable	considerable
la différence	difference
l'élément (m.)	element
la gloire	glory
l'opération (f.)	operation
le parent	parent
royal	royal
la sorte	sort

LESSON 7

6. GOOD MORNING!

(Good Morning!)

Bonjour.	Hello! Good morning. Good afternoon. ("Good day.")[1]
Monsieur	Mr.
Monsieur Lenoir	Mr. Lenoir
Bonjour, Monsieur Lenoir.	Good morning (Good afternoon), Mr. Lenoir.
Bonsoir.	Good evening.
Madame	Madam
Madame Lenoir	Mrs. Lenoir
Bonsoir, Madame Lenoir.	Good evening, Mrs. Lenoir.
bonne	good
nuit	night
Bonne nuit, Madame Lenoir.	Good night, Mrs. Lenoir.
comment	how
allez-vous	are you ("do you go")
Comment allez-vous?	How are you? How do you do?
Mademoiselle	Miss
Mademoiselle Lenoir	Miss Lenoir
Comment allez-vous, Mademoiselle Lenoir?	How do you do, Miss Lenoir?
très	very
bien	well

[1] Words in parentheses and quotation marks are literal translations.

Trés bien.	Very well.
Merci.	Thank you. Thanks.
Très bien, merci.	Very well, thanks.
Et vous?	And you?
Merci, très bien.	Very well, thanks.
parlez	speak
lentement	slowly
Parlez lentement.	Speak slowly.
s'il vous plaît	please
Parlez lentement, s'il vous plaît.	Please speak slowly.
Répétez.	Repeat.
Répétez, s'il vous plaît.	Please repeat.
merci	thanks
beaucoup	much, a lot
Merci beaucoup.	Thank you very much. Thanks a lot.
il n'y a	you're welcome
pas de quoi	("it isn't anything")
Il n'y a pas de quoi.	Not at all.
Je vous remercie.	Thank you.
Je vous en remercie.	Thank you for it.
De rien.	Not at all.
A demain.	Till tomorrow. See you tomorrow.
A samedi.	Till Saturday. See you Saturday.
A lundi.	Till Monday. See you Monday.

A jeudi.	Till Thursday. See you Thursday.
A ce soir.	Till this evening. See you this evening.
A demain soir.	Till tomorrow evening. See you tomorrow evening.
A la semaine prochaine.	Till next week. See you next week.
A bientôt.	See you soon.
A tout à l'heure.	See you later. See you in a little while.
Au revoir.	Good-by.

QUIZ 2

1. *très bien*	1. speak
2. *bonsoir*	2. how
3. *parlez*	3. much, a lot
4. *merci*	4. see you tomorrow (until tomorrow)
5. *comment*	5. How are you?
6. *s'il vous plaît*	6. very well
7. *beaucoup*	7. slowly
8. *à demain*	8. thank you
9. *Comment allez-vous?*	9. please
10. *lentement*	10. good evening

ANSWERS

1—6; 2—10; 3—1; 4—8; 5—2; 6—9; 7—3; 8—4; 9—5; 10—7.

LESSON 8

7. DO YOU HAVE . . . ?

(What Do You Have to Eat?)

Avez-vous . . .?	Do you have . . .?
de l'eau	some water
des cigarettes	some (any) cigarettes
de feu	a light
des allumettes	some matches
du savon	some soap
du papier	some paper

Notice that "some" or "any" is translated by *de* "of" (other forms of *de* are *du, des, d';* see page 44) and that in many cases French uses *de* (for example, *du feu)* where we don't use "some" or "any" in English.

8. WHAT DO YOU HAVE TO EAT?

le petit déjeuner	breakfast
le déjeuner	lunch
le dîner	dinner, supper
Vous désirez . . .?	What will you have? ("You wish . . .?")
Bonjour, Monsieur[1] vous désirez . . .?	Good afternoon. What would you like?
Donnez-moi . . .	Give me . . .
Donnez-moi la carte	Give me a menu. Let me have a menu.

[1]In French you add Monsieur (Madame, Mademoiselle) when addressing a stranger.

Je voudrais . . .	I'd like . . .
du pain	some bread
du beurre	some butter
de la soupe	some soup
de la viande	some meat
du boeuf	some beef
des oeufs	some eggs
des légumes	some vegetables
des pommes de terre	some potatoes
de la salade	some salad
du lait	some milk
du vin	some wine
du sucre	some sugar
du sel	some salt
du poivre	some pepper
Apportez-moi . . .	Bring me . . .
une cuillère	a spoon
une cuillère à café	a teaspoon
une fourchette	a fork
un couteau	a knife
une serviette	a napkin
une assiette	a plate
un verre	a glass
Je voudrais . . .	I'd like . . .
un verre d'eau	a glass of water
une tasse de thé	a cup of tea
une tasse de café	a cup of coffee
une bouteille de vin rouge	a bottle of red wine
une bouteille de vin blanc	a bottle of white wine
encore un oeuf	another egg
un peu de cela	a little of that
encore un peu de cela	a little more of that

encore du pain	some more bread
encore un peu de pain	a little more bread
encore de la viande	some more meat
encore un peu de viande	a little more meat
L'addition, s'il vous plaît.	The check, please.

QUIZ 3

1. *viande*	1. Bring me . . .
2. *vin rouge*	2. matches
3. *Avez-vous . . . ?*	3. Give me . . .
4. *lait*	4. meat
5. *beurre*	5. some water
6. *Donnez-moi . . .*	6. a light
7. *allumettes*	7. milk
8. *encore du pain*	8. eggs
9. *Apportez-moi . . .*	9. red wine
10. *de l'eau*	10. The check, please.
11. *de feu*	11. Do you have . . . ?
12. *du sel*	12. butter
13. *des oeufs*	13. a cup of coffee
14. *une tasse de café*	14. some more bread
15. *L'addition, s'il vous plait.*	15. some salt

ANSWERS

1—4; 2—9; 3—11; 4—7; 5—12; 6—3; 7—2; 8—14; 9—1; 10—5; 11—6; 12—15; 13—8; 14—13; 15—10.

LESSON 9

9. COMMON VERB FORMS[1]

(Common Verb Forms)

1. I give

je donne	I give, I'm giving
tu donnes	you (*fam.*) give, you are giving
il donne	he gives, he's giving
elle donne	she gives, she's giving
on donne	one gives, one is giving; they (people) give, they (people) are giving
nous donnons	we give, we're giving
vous donnez	you give, you're giving
ils donnent	they give, they're giving (*masc.*)
elles donnent	they give, they're giving (*fem.*)

NOTES

a. Notice the endings:

je	-e	nous	-ons
tu	-es	vous	-ez
il	-e	ils	-ont

b. These forms, which make up "the present tense," translate English "I give," "I'm giving" and "I do give."

[1] This lesson and several of the following lessons are longer than the others. They contain the grammatical information you need to know from the start. Don't try to memorize anything. Read each section until you understand every point and then as you continue with the course try to observe examples of the points mentioned. Refer back to the grammatical sections as often as necessary. In this way you will eventually find that you have a good grasp of the basic features of French grammar without any deliberate memorizing of "rules."

c. *Tu donnes* is used to people you know well (whom you call by their first name in English—members of one's family and close friends) and to children, pets, etc. *Vous donnez* is used to several people or to someone you don't know very well (whom you wouldn't call by his first name in English). The *tu* form is called the "familiar" form, the *vous* form the "polite" or "formal."

d. *Il donne* means "he gives" or "it gives." "They give" is translated *ils donnent* when referring to men (or to masculine nouns) and *elles donnent* when referring to women (or to feminine nouns).

e. *On donne* means "one gives." It can be translated several ways in English: "they give," "people give," "it's given," etc.

f. Notice that as far as the sound is concerned there are only three endings:

1) je donne

{ *tu donnes* *il donne* *on donne* *ils donnent*	all pronounced *donn* whether spelled *donne*, *donnes*, or *donnent*.

2) nous donn-ons

3) vous donn-ez

2. Give!

Donne! Give! (the familiar form used to people one knows well; compare *tu donnes* above)

Donnez!	Give! (the polite form; compare *vous donnez* above)
Ne donne pas!	Don't give (familiar)
Ne donnez pas!	Don't give! (polite)

This form of the verb which is used in commands and requests is called "the imperative."

Notice that "not" ("Do not give!" "Don't give!") is *ne . . . pas*.

3. I speak

je parle	I speak, I'm speaking
tu parles	you speak, you're speaking (familiar)
il parle	he speaks, he's speaking
nous parlons	we speak, we're speaking
vous parlez	you speak, you're speaking
ils parlent	they speak, they're speaking
Parle	Speak! (familiar)
Parlez!	Speak! (polite)

4. I don't give

je donne	I give
je ne donne pas	I don't give

je ne donne pas	I don't give	
tu ne donnes pas	you don't give	(familiar)
il ne donne pas	he doesn't give	
nous ne donnons pas	we don't give	
vous ne donnez pas	you don't give	
ils ne donnent pas	they don't give	

10. ASKING A QUESTION

1. To ask a question you reverse the order:

Vous donnez.	You give. You're giving.
Donnez-vous?	Do you give? Are you giving?
Donnes-tu?[1]	Do you *(fam.)* give?
Donne-t-il?[2]	Does he give?
Donne-t-elle?	Does she give?
Donnons-nous?	Do we give?
Donnez-vous?	Do you give?
Donnent-ils?	Do they give?

2. Another way of asking a question is to put *est-ce que* . . . before the statement:

Est-ce que je donne?	Do I give?
Est-ce que tu donnes?	Do you (*fam.*) give?
Est-ce qu'il donne?	Does he give?
Est-ce qu'elle donne?	Does she give?
Est-ce qu'on donne	Does one (they, people) give?
Est-ce que nous donnons?	Do we give?
Est-ce que vous donnez?	Do you give?
Est-ce qu'ils donnent?	Do they give?
Est-ce qu'elles donnent?	Do they give?
Est-ce que je ne donne pas?	Don't I give?
Est-ce que tu ne donnes pas?	Don't you (*fam.*) give?

[1] The form *Donne-je?* "Do I give?" is not used; *Est-ce que je donne?* is used instead (see above).

[2] Notice that you insert a *t*.

Est-ce u'il ne donne pas?	Doesn't he give?
Est-ce qu'elle ne donne pas?	Doesn't she give?
Est-ce qu'on ne donne pas?	Doesn't one (they, people) give?
Est-ce que nous ne donnons pas?	Don't we give?
Est-ce que vous ne donnez pas?	Don't you give?
Est-ce qu'ils ne donnent pas?	Don't they give?
Est-ce qu'elles ne donnent pas?	Don't they give?

REVIEW QUIZ 1

Choose the correct French word equivalent to the English.

1. Five =
   a. six
   b. sep
   c. cinq

2. Eight =
   a. huit
   b. neuf
   c. quatre

3. Tuesday =
   a. mercredi
   b. mardi
   c. vendredi

4. Sunday =
   a. dimanche
   b. samedi
   c. lundi

5. August =
   a. août
   b. septembre
   c. avril

6. June =
   a. juillet
   b. juin
   c. mai

7. Red =
   a. bleu
   b. orange
   c. rouge

8. Green =
   a. jaune
   b. vert
   c. gris

9. Black =
   a. noir
   b. marron
   c. blanc

10. Brown =
    a. noir
    b. rouge
    c. brun

11. Good Morning =
    a. bonjour
    b. bonsoir
    c. comment

12. Very well =
    a. merci
    b. très bien
    c. très

13. Thank you =
    a. bien
    b. merci
    c. très

14. Please =
    a. parlez
    b. merci
    c. s'il vous plaît

15. Good-by =
    a. à demain
    b. au revoir
    c. bonjour

16. He gives =
    a. il donne
    b. elle donne
    c. ils donnet

17. We are speaking =
    a. nous parlons
    b. vous parlez
    c. nous donnons

18. I don't give =
    a. il ne donne pas
    b. je donne
    c. je ne donne pas

19. Do you give? =
    a. Donnez-vous?
    b. Donne-t-il?
    c. Donne-t-on?

20. Do I give? =
    a. Est-ce que vous donnez?
    b. Est-ce que je donne?
    c. Est-ce qu'il donne?

ANSWERS

1—c.; 2—a.; 3—b.; 4—a.; 5—a.; 6—b.; 7—c.; 8—b.; 9—a.; 10—c.; 11—a.; 12—b.; 13—b.; 14—c.; 15—b.; 16—a.; 17—a.; 18—c; 19—a.; 20—b.

LESSON 10

11. LINKING OF SOUNDS

When words are closely connected grammatically in French they are also closely connected in pronunciation, so that if the first word ends in the consonant and the second begins with a vowel the consonant is carried over and begins the second word:

u—nexemple[1]	an example
pa—rexemple	for example

There are many cases where the first words ends in a consonant which is not pronounced when the word is used by itself or before a word beginning with a consonant *(vous* pronounced *vou)* but which is pronounced when the following word begins with a vowel or *h (vous avez* pronounced *vou-zavez).* When this "linking" takes place:

s is pronounced *z*—*vous avez (vou-zavez)* you have
les amis (lay-zamis) the friends

x is pronounced *z*—*aux Etats-Unis (au-zEtat-zUnis)* to the United States
deux amis (deu-zamis) *two friends*

[1]The dash shows that the *n* goes with the next word: *u-nexemple.*

d is pronounced *t*—*un grand enfant (un gran-tenfant)* a big child
un grand homme (un gran-thomme) a great (important) man

(Asking Your Way I)

Other Examples:

Il est.	He is.
Est-il?	Is he?
Est-elle?	Is she?
Ils sont.	They are.
Sont-ils?	Are they *(masc.)?*
Sont-elles?	Are they *(fem.)?*
C'est . . .	It is . . .
C'est à moi.	It's mine.
C'est ici.	It's here.
Nous avons.	We have.
Vous avez.	You have.
Ils ont.	They have.
Les amis.	The friends.
Deux amis.	Two friends.
Les élèves.	The pupils.
Pas encore.	Not yet.
Très intéressant.	Very interesting.
Après une heure.	After an hour.
Venez-ici.	Come here.
Allez-y.	Go there.
Un petit enfant.	A small child.
Un grand enfant.	A big child.
Je suis ici.	I'm here.
Ils sont allés.	They went.
Chez eux.	At their home.
Sans intérêt	Without interest.

12. ASKING YOUR WAY

1. Where?

Pardon, monsieur.	Excuse me. May I trouble you?
où	where
est	is
Où est-il?	Where is it (he)?
l'hôtel	the hotel
Où est l'hôtel?	Where is the hotel?
Où est le restaurant?	Where is the restaurant?
Où est le téléphone?	Where is the telephone?
Pouvez-vous me dire . . .	Can you tell me . . .
Pouvez-vous me dire où est le téléphone?	Can you tell me where the telephone is?
Pouvez-vous me dire où est la gare?	Can you tell me where the (railroad) station is?

Où est is the simplest way of saying "Where is" but it is more idiomatic to say: *Où se trouve* . . . ("Where does it find itself . . .?")

Où se trouve l'hôtel?	Where is the hotel? ("Where does the hotel find itself?")
Pouvez-vous me dire où se trouve la poste?	Can you tell me where the post office is?
Pouvez-vous me dire où se trouve le téléphone?	Can you tell me where the telephone is?

2. Here and There.

Ici.	Here.
Là.	There.
Là bas.	Over there.
Par où est-ce?	Which way is it?
Par ici.	This way.
Par là.	That way.
Par là-bas.	Over that way.
C'est par ici.	It's this way.
C'est par là-bas.	It's over that way.

LESSON 11

(Asking Your Way II)

A droite.	To the right.
A gauche.	To the left.
A votre droite.	To your right.
A votre gauche.	To your left.
Sur votre gauche.	On your left.
C'est à droite.	It's to the right.
C'est à gauche.	It's to the left.
Tournez à droite.	Turn right.
Tournez à gauche.	Turn left.
Continuez tout droit.	Keep straight on.
C'est tout droit.	It's straight ahead.
C'est tout droit devant vous.	It's straight ahead of you.
Allez tout droit.	Go straight ahead.
C'est en face.	It's directly opposite.
C'est en haut.	It's above.
C'est en bas.	It's below.
C'est au coin.	It's on the corner.
Ce n'est pas ici.	It's not here.
Ce n'est pas là.	It's not there.

C'est ici.	It's here.
Ce n'est pas ici.	It's not here.
C'est là.	It's there.
C'est là-bas.	It's over there.
C'est là-haut.	It's up there.
Il est ici.	He's here.
Venez ici.	Come here.
Restez ici.	Stay here.
Attendez là.	Wait there.
Allez par ici.	Go this way.
Allez par là.	Go that way.
Qui est là?	Who's there?
Mettez-le ici.	Put it here.
Mettez-le là.	Put it there.

3. Near and Far.

Près.	Near.
Près d'ici.	Near here.
Tout près.	Very near. Quite close.
Près du village.	Near the village.
Près de la route.	Near the road.
Près du lui.	Near him.
C'est tout près.	It's very near.
C'est tout près d'ici.	It's very near here.
Loin.	Far.
C'est loin? / **Est-ce loin?**	Is it far?
C'est loin.	It's far.
Ce n'est pas loin.	It's not far.
C'est loin d'ici.	It's far from here.

4. There.

Y.	There. To there.
Est-il à Paris?	Is he in Paris?
Oui, il y est.	Yes, he is (there).

Paul, est-il là?	Is Paul there?
Oui, il y est.	Yes, he's there.
Va-t-il à Paris?	Is he going to Paris?
Oui, il y va.	Yes, he's going there.
J'y vais.	I'm going there.
Je ne veux pas y aller.	I don't want to go there.
J'y demeure.	I live there.

QUIZ 4

1. *Pouvez-vous me dire où est le téléphone?*	1. It's this way.
2. *Où se trouve l'hôtel?*	2. It's to the right.
3. *C'est par ici.*	3. Turn left.
4. *C'est tout droit.*	4. It's (directly) opposite.
5. *C'est à droite.*	5. It's straight ahead.
6. *J'y demeure.*	6. Can you tell me where the telephone is?
7. *Attendez là.*	7. Where is the hotel? ("Where does the hotel find itself?")
8. *Allez par ici.*	8. I live there.
9. *Tournez à gauche.*	9. It's not here.
10. *C'est en face.*	10. Stay here.
11. *Ce n'est pas loin.*	11. Wait there.
12. *Mettez-le là.*	12. Go this way.
13. *Ce n'est pas ici.*	13. Who's there?
14. *Restez ici.*	14. Put it there.
15. *Qui est là?*	15. It's not far.

ANSWERS

1—6; 2—7; 3—1; 4—5; 5—2; 6—8; 7—11; 8—12; 9—3; 10—4; 11—15; 12—14; 13—9; 14—10; 15—13.

WORD STUDY

comédie	comedy
constant	constant
contraire	contrary
désir	desire
long	long
nord	north
oncle	uncle
organe	organ
poste	post
simple	simple

LESSON 12

13. THE AND A

1. *le (la)* "the."

Je donne le livre à un enfant.	I give (I'm giving) the book to a child.
Il donne la lettre à une femme.	He gives (he's giving) the letter to a woman.
Nous donnons les livres à un garçon.	We give (we're giving) the books to a boy.
Vous donnez les lettres à ma fille.	You give (you're giving) the letters to my daughter.

Notice that the book is *le livre,* the letter is *la lettre.* Nouns that take *le* are called "masculine," nouns that take *la* are called "feminine." In the plural, however, both have *les:*

les livres	the books
les lettres	the letters

2. *un (une)* "a."

Nouns that take *le* (masculine nouns) take *un:*

un livre	a book
un garçon	a boy

Nouns that take *la* (feminine nouns) take *une:*

une lettre	a letter
une femme	a woman

3. *le (la)* before vowels.

Je parle à l'ami de Jean.	I'm talking to John's friend.
Il donne la lettre à l'amie de Jeanne.	He gives (he's giving) the letter to Jean's (girl) friend.
Nous entrons à l'hôtel.	We went into the hotel.
Je marche sur l'herbe.	I'm walking on the grass.

Notice that when *le* or *la* comes before a vowel or *h* it becomes *l':*

l'ami	the friend
l'homme	the man

Other Examples:

l'heure	the hour	*les heures*	the hours
l'hôtel	the hotel	*les hôtels*	the hotels

14. MASCULINE AND FEMININE

un ami de Jean	John's friend ("a friend of John")
une amie de Jeanne	Jean's (girl) friend

Notice that *e* is often added to a masculine word to make it feminine:

un ami *une amie*

Other Examples:

MASCULINE		FEMININE	
grand	big	*grande*	big
petit	small	*petite*	small
étudiant	male student	*étudiante*	female student
client	customer	*cliente*	woman customer

15. POSITIONS OF ADJECTIVES

1. Adjectives usually follow the noun:

un livre français	a French book
un homme intéressant	an interesting man
une idée excellente	an excellent idea

2. A number of common adjectives, however, usually precede the noun:

autre	other	*gros*	big
beau	beautiful	*jeune*	young
bon	good	*joli*	pretty
court	short	*long*	long
gentil	nice, pleasant	*mauvais*	bad
		nouveau	new
grand	great, large, tall	*petit*	small, little
		vieux	old

16. PLURAL

1. The plural of most nouns ends in *-s:*

le livre	the book	*les livres*	the books
la lettre	the letter	*les lettres*	the letters

Since the *s* is not pronounced there is no difference in speech between *livre* "book" and *livres* "books." The difference between singular and plural is clear, however, as soon as you add *le* or *les:*

le livre	the book	*les livres*	the books

2. The plural of most adjectives ends in *-s:*

je suis prêt	I'm ready
elle est prête	she's ready
nous sommes prêts	we're ready
elles sont prêtes	they're ready

17. OF AND TO

OF

1. *de* "of"

la lettre de mon ami	my friend's letter (the letter of my friend)
le livre de Jean	John's book
les livres de l'élève	the pupil's books

2. *de la* "of the" *(fem.)*

la lettre de la jeune fille	the girl's letter
Donnez-moi de la viande.	Give me some meat.

3. *de l'* "of the" *(before vowels and h)*

le livre de l'ami	the friend's book
l'entrée de l'hôtel	the hotel's entrance
Donnez-moi de l'argent.	Give me some money.
Donnez-moi de l'eau.	Give me some water.

Notice that *de* is used in some cases where in English we use the possessive (John's book) and in other cases where we use the word "some" (Give me some water).

4. *du* "of the" *(masc.)*

le livre de père	the father's book
le livre du garçon	the boy's book

Notice that *de + le = du.*

5. *des* "of the" *(pl.)*

les rues des villes	the streets of the towns
les livres des élèves	the pupils' books (the books of the pupils)
Donnez-moi des pommes de terre.	Give me some potatoes.

TO

1. *à* "to"

Je vais à Paris.	I'm going to Paris.

2. *à la* "to the" *(fem.)*

Je donne la lettre à la mère.	I give (I'm giving) the letter to the mother.
Portez cette valise à la gare.	Carry (take) this valise to the station.

3. *à l'* "to the" *(before a vowel or h)*

Donnez-le à l'enfant.	Give it to the child.
Je donne la lettre à l'ami de Jean.	I give (I'm giving) the letter to John's friend.
Il va à l'hôpital.	He's going to the hospital.

4. *au* "to the" *(masc.)*

Je donne la lettre au père.	I give (I'm giving) the letter to the father.
Je vais au théâtre.	I'm going to the theater.
Il va au cinéma.	He's going to the movies.

Notice that *a + le = aux.*

5. *aux* "to the" *(pl.)*

Il donne de l'argent aux pauvres.	He gives money to the poor.
Je vais aux concerts de l'orchestre symphonique.	I'm going to the symphony concerts.

Notice that *a + les = aux.*

WORK STUDY

la chaîne	chain
complet	complete
la crème	cream
le désert	desert
éternel	eternal
la fontaine	fountain
la lettre	letter
l'officier (m.)	officer
le système	system
le télégraphe	telegraph

18. TO BE OR NOT TO BE

About 4000 to 4500 verbs in common use have the forms given for *donner* and *parler* (the "regular verbs"). Among some of the verbs which do not follow this pattern (the "irregular verbs") there are some extremely common ones, such as:

être	to be
avoir	to have
aller	to go
venir	to come
faire	to do
dire	to say

TO BE

(To Be or Not to Be)

1. I Am, You Are, He Is.

je suis	I am
tu es	you are *(fam.)*
il est	he is
elle est	she is
on est	one is
nous sommes	we are
vous êtes	you are *(pl.)*
ils sont	they are *(masc.)*
elles sont	they are *(fem.)*

NOT TO BE

2. I Am Not, You Are Not.

Je ne suis pas	I am not
tu n'es pas	you are not
il n'est pas	he is not
elle n'est pas	she is not
on n'est pas	one is not

nous ne sommes pas	we are not
vous n'êtes pas	you are not
ils ne sont pas	they are not
elles ne sont pas	they are not
Soyez!	Be!
Soyez tranquille.	Be quiet. Don't worry.
Je suis américain.	I'm (an) American.
Je suis dans la chambre.	I'm in the room.
Je suis à l'hôtel.	I'm at the hotel.
Il est ici.	He's here.
Elle est là.	She's there.
Ils sont ici.	They're *(masc.)* here.
Elles sont là-bas.	They're *(fem.)* over there.
Je suis prêt.	I'm ready.
Elle est prête.	She's ready.
Ils sont prêts.	They're *(masc.)* ready.
Elles sont prêtes.	They're *(fem.)* ready.
Etes-vous certain, Monsieur?	Are you certain, sir?
Etes-vous certaine, Madame?	Are you certain, madam?
Etes-vous certaine, Mademoiselle?	Are you certain, miss?
Etes-vous certains, Messieurs?	Are you certain, gentlemen?
Etes-vous certaines, Mesdames?	Are you certain? *(to several married women)*
Etes-vous certaines, Mesdemoiselles?	Are you certain? *(to several unmarried women)*
Etes-vous anglais?	Are you English?
Oui, je suis anglais.	Yes, I'm English.

Oui, je le suis.	Yes, I am. (Note that in French you add *le* "it".)
Non, je ne suis pas anglais.	No, I'm not English.
Non, je ne le suis pas.	No, I'm not.
Quelle heure est-il?	What time is it?
D'où êtes-vous?	Where are you from?
Je suis de Paris.	I'm from Paris.

3. Am I? Are You?

suis-je? or *est-ce que je suis?*	Am I?
es-tu?	Are you?
est-il?	Is he?
est-elle?	Is she?
sommes-nous?	Are we?
êtes-vous?	Are you?
sont-ils?	Are they *(masc.)?*
sont-elles?	Are they *(fem.)?*

4. Where am I?

Où suis-je?	Where am I?
Où es-tu?	Where are you?
Où est-il?	Where is he?
Où est-elle?	Where is she?
Où sommes-nous?	Where are we?
Où êtes-vous?	Where are you?
Où sont-ils?	Where are they *(masc.)?*
Où sont-elles?	Where are they *(fem.)?*

19. MY, YOUR, HIS

Où est mon livre?	Where is my book?
Où est ton livre?	Where is your *(familiar)* book?
Où est son livre?	Where is his (her) book?
Où est notre livre?	Where is our book?
Où est votre livre?	Where is your *(polite)* book?
Où est leur livre?	Where is their book?
Où est ma lettre?	Where is my letter?
Où est ta lettre?	Where is your *(familiar)* letter?
Où est sa lettre?	Where is his (her) letter?
Où est notre lettre?	Where is our letter?
Où est votre lettre?	Where is your *(polite)* letter?
Où est leur lettre?	Where is their letter?
Où sont mes livres?	Where are my books?
Où sont tes livres?	Where are your *(familiar)* books?
Où sont ses livres?	Where are his (her) books?
Où sont nos livres?	Where are our books?
Où sont vos livres?	Where are your *(polite)* books?
Où sont leurs livres?	Where are their books?
Où sont mes lettres?	Where are my letters?
Où sont tes lettres?	Where are your *(familiar)* letters?
Où sont ses lettres?	Where are his (her) letters?

Où sont nos lettres?	Where are our letters?
Où sont vos lettres?	Where are your *(polite)* letters?
Où sont leurs lettres?	Where are their letters?

Notice that my (your, his, etc.) is *mon* before masculine nouns and *ma* before feminine nouns but that in the plural the same form *(mes)* is used before both masculine and feminine nouns. Notice also that the *mon (ma,* etc.) agrees in gender with the following noun rather than with the subject: In *Où est sa lettre?* "Where is his letter?" *sa* is feminine because *lettre* is feminine (even though "his" refers to a man).

QUIZ 5

1. D'où êtes-vous?	1. What time is it?
2. Quelle heure est-il?	2. Where are you from?
3. Il est ici.	3. Where is he?
4. Je suis prêt.	4. Where is his letter?
5. Etes-vous certain?	5. They are ready.
6. Où est-il?	6. Where are their books?
7. Où est sa lettre?	7. I'm ready.
8. Où sont leurs livres?	8. I'm at the hotel.
9. Elles sont prêtes.	9. Are you certain?
10. Soyez tranquille.	10. He's here.
11. Je suis à l'hôtel.	11. I'm (an) American.
12. Je suis américain.	12. Don't worry.
13. Je ne suis pas.	13. I'm from Paris.
14. Nous sommes.	14. I'm not.
15. Je suis de Paris.	15. We are.

ANSWERS

1—2; 2—1; 3—10; 4—7; 5—9; 6—3; 7—4; 8—6; 9—5; 10—12; 11—8; 12—11; 13—14; 14—15; 15—13.

LESSON 13

20. IT IS

(Asking a Question)

C'est bon. It's good.
Ce n'est pas bon. It's no good.
C'est bien. It's (that's) all right. ("It's well.")
Ce n'est pas bien. It's not very good (nice). It's not right (fair).
C'est mal. It's bad.
Ce n'est pas mal. It's not bad.
C'est petit. It's small.
C'est grand. It's big.
Ce n'est rein. It's nothing.
C'est difficile. It's hard (difficult).
C'est facile. It's easy.
C'est très facile.[1] It's very easy.
C'est assez facile. It's easy enough.
C'est plus facile. It's easier.
C'est moins difficile. It's less difficult.
C'est loin. It's far.
Ce n'est pas très loin. It's not very far.
C'est près d'ici. It's near here.
C'est très près d'ici. It's very near here.
C'est peu. It's (a) little.
C'est trop peu. It's too little.
C'est assez. It's enough.
C'est beaucoup. It's a lot.
C'est là. It's there.
C'est là-bas. It's over there.
Ce n'est pas là. It's not there.
C'est ici. It's here.

[1] The recording erroneously says, "C'est plus facile."

Ce n'est pas ici.	It's not here.
C'est par ici.	It's this way.
C'est par là.	It's that way.
C'est pour moi.	It's for me.
C'est pour toi.	It's for him (fam.).
C'est pour lui.	It's for him.
C'est pour elle.	It's for her.
C'est pour nous.	It's for us.
C'est pour vous.	It's for you.
C'estpour eux.	It's for them.
Ce n'est pas pour eux.	It's not for them.
C'est pour les enfants.	It's for the children.
C'est ceci.	This is it.
C'est cela.	That's it. That's right.
C'est ça.	That's it. That's right.

21. ASKING A QUESTION II

There are several ways of asking a question:

1. Reverse the order.
2. *Est-ce que . . .* with the regular word order.
3. Regular word order with the question intonation (that is, with the pitch of the voice raised at the end of the sentence).

Est-ce ceci?	Is it this?
Est-ce cela?	Is it that?
Est-ce que c'est cela?	Is it that?
Il est ici.	He's here.
Est-il ici? **Est-ce qu'il est ici?**	Is he here?
C'est vrai.	It's true.
C'est vrai?	It's true?
Est-ce vrai? **Est-ce que c'est vrai?**	It is true?

Où est-il? **Où est-ce qu'il est?**	Where is he?
Où est'ce? **Où est-ce que c'est?**	Where is it?
Est-il prêt? **Est-ce qu'il est prêt?**	Is he ready?
Etes-vous prêt? **Est-ce que vous êtes prêt?**	Are you ready?
Sont-ils prêts? **Est-ce qu'ils sont prêts?**	Are they *(masc.)* ready?
Sont-elles prêtes? **Est-ce qu'elles sont prêtes?**	Are they *(fem.)* ready?
Venez-vouz? **Est-ce que vous venez?**	Are you coming?
Avez-vous des cigarettes? **Est-ce que vous avez des cigarettes?**	Do you have any cigarettes?
Avez-vous du feu? **Est-ce que vous avez du feu?**	Do you have a light?
Parlez-vous anglais? **Est-ce que vous parlez anglais?**	Do you speak English?
Parlez-vous français? **Est-ce que vous parlez français?**	Do you speak French?

WORD STUDY

la bande	band
le chauffeur	chauffeur
commun	common
la composition	composition
la conscience	conscience
la décoration	decoration
la description	description
la mission	mission
le numéro	numeral
la région	region

LESSON 14

22. TO HAVE AND HAVE NOT

(To Have and Have Not)

AVOIR to have

1. I Have.

j'ai	I have
tu as	you have
il a	he has
nous avons	we have
vous avez	you have
ils ont	they have

2. I Don't Have.

je n'ai pas	I don't have, I haven't
tu n'as pas	you don't have, *etc.*
il n'a pas	he doesn't have
nous n'avons pas	we don't have
vous n'avez pas	you don't have
ils n'ont pas	they don't have

J'ai ceci.	I have this. I've got this.

Je n'ai rien.	I have nothing. I don't have anything. There's nothing wrong with me.
J'ai de l'argent.	I have money.
J'ai assez d'argent.	I have enough money.
Je n'ai pas d'argent.	I haven't any money.
J'ai assez de temps.	I have enough time.
Ils n'ont pas de cigarettes.	They don't have any cigarettes.
J'ai faim.	I'm hungry.
Il a faim.	He's hungry.
J'ai soif.	I'm thirsty.
Il a froid.	He's cold.
Nous avons froid.	We're cold.
Il a chaud.	He's hot.
Avez-vous chaud?	Are you hot?
Il a raison.	He's right.
Il a tort.	He's wrong.
Vous avez raison.	You're right.
Elle a peur.	She's afraid.
J'ai besoin . . .	I need . . .
J'ai besoin de cela.	I need that.
Il a besoin de ceci.	He needs this.
J'ai vingt ans.	I'm twenty (years old).
Il a trente ans.	He is thirty (years old).
J'ai mal aux dents.	I have a toothache.
Elle a mal à la tête.	She has a headache.

3. Do I Have?

ai-je?	do I have?
as-tu?	do you have?
a-t-il?	does he have?
avons-nous?	do we have?

avez-vous?	do you have?
ont-ils?	do they have?

4. Don't I Have?

n'ai-je pas?	don't I have? haven't I?
n'as-tu-pas?	don't you have?
n'a-t-il pas?	doesn't he have?
n'avons-nous pas?	don't we have?
n'avez-vous pas?	don't you have?
n'ont-ils pas?	don't they have?
A-t-il de l'argent?	Does he have any money?
A-t-elle assez d'argent	Does she have enough money?
Ai-je-besoin de cela?	Do I need that?
Avons-nous besoin de ceci?	Do we need this?
A-t-il des amis à Paris?	Does he have (any) friends in Paris?
Avez-vous un crayon?	Do you have a pencil?
Avez-vous un stylo?	Do you have a pen?
Avez-vous un timbre?	Do you have a stamp?
Avez-vous du papier?	Do you have any paper?
Avez-vous des cigarettes? / **Est-ce que vous avez des cigarettes?**	Do you have any cigarettes?
Avez-vous du feu?	Do you have a light?
Avez-vous une allumette?	Do you have a match?
Qu'avez-vous?	What's the matter with you? What hurts you?

Qu'est-ce qu'il a?	What's the matter with him?
Quel âge avez-vous?	How old are you?
Combien en avez-vous?	How many of them do you have?
Avez-vous le temps de me parler?	Do you have time to talk to me?

LESSON 15

23. SOME WORDS AND IDIOMS

(Some Words and Idioms)

1. There Is.

Il y a . . .	There is. There are.
Il y en a.	There's some (of it).
Il n'y a rien.	There's nothing.
Il n'y a plus de cela.	There's no more (of that).
Il n'y en a plus.	There isn't any more (of it).
Il n'y a pas de quoi.	Not at all. Don't mention it.
Il n'y a pas de réponse.	There's no answer.
Il n'y a pas de différence.	There's no difference.
Il n'y a aucune difficulté.	There's no difficulty.
Il n'y a personne.	There's nobody.
Il n'y a personne ici.	There's nobody here.
Y a-t-il des lettres pour moi?	Are there any letters for me?
Y a-t-il du courrier?	Is there any mail?
Y a-t-il du courrier pour moi?	Is there any mail for me?
Y a-t-il beaucoup de monde?	Is there a crowd? Are there a lot of people?

Y a-t-il le téléphone ici?	Is there a telephone here?
Est-ce qu'il y a un restaurant près d'ici?	Is there a restaurant near here?
Est-ce qu'il y a une pharmacie près d'ici?	Is there a drugstore near here?
Est-ce qu'il y a un café près d'ici?	Is there a café near here?
Il y a quatre personnes ici.	There are four people here.

2. Ago.

Il y a . . .	Ago.
Il y a une heure.	An hour ago.
Il y a deux heures.	Two hours ago.
Il y a trois heures.	Three hours ago.
Il y a un jour.	A day ago.
Il y a deux jours.	Two days ago.
Il y a trois semaines.	Three weeks ago.
Il y a cinq mois.	Five months ago.
Il y a cinq ans.	Five years ago.
Il y a dix ans.	Ten years ago.
Il y a longtemps.	A long time ago.
Il y a assez longtemps.	A rather long time ago.
Il n'y a pas longtemps.	Not so long ago.
Il y a peu de temps.	A short time ago.

3. Also.

Aussi.	Also, too.
Moi aussi.	I also (too).
Toi aussi.	You *(fam.)* also (too).
Lui aussi.	He also (too).
Elle aussi.	She also (too).
Nous aussi.	We also (too).
Vous aussi.	You also (too).
Eux aussi.	They also (too).

Il vient aussi.	He's also coming.
Ils viennent aussi.	They're also coming.
Il l'a fait aussi.	He also did it.
Moi aussi je viens.	I'm also coming.
Ils sont aussi grands que les autres.	They're as tall as the others.
Ils ne sont pas aussi petits que les autres.	They're not as small as the others.
Ce n'est pas aussi bon que l'autre.	That's not as good as the other.
Ce n'est pas aussi grand que l'autre.	That's not as large as the other.
Venez aussi vite que possible.	Come as quickly as you can.
Faites-le aussi vite que possible.	Do it as soon as possible.
Faites-le aussi bien que possible.	Do it as well as possible.

QUIZ 6

1. *J'ai assez de temps.*	1. Not at all. Don't mention it.
2. *Il a raison.*	2. There's no answer.
3. *J' ai besoin de cela.*	3. There's no difference.
4. *Il a tort.*	4. There's no difficulty.
5. *Il a froid.*	5. Are there any letters for me?
6. *J'ai faim.*	6. There's nobody here.
7. *J'ai vingt ans.*	7. A day ago.
8. *J'ai soif.*	8. Three weeks ago.
9. *Quel âge avez-vous?*	9. A long time ago.
10. *A-t-il de l'argent?*	10. Come as quickly as you can.

11. *Combien en avez-vous?*	11. I have nothing. I don't have anything. There's nothing wrong with me.
12. *A-t-il des amis à Paris?*	12. I have enough time.
13. *Je n'ai rien.*	13. I'm hungry.
14. *Vous avez raison.*	14. I'm thirsty.
15. *Qu'est-ce qu'il a?*	15. He's cold.
16. *Il y a trois semaines.*	16. He's right.
17. *Il n'y a pas de différence.*	17. He's wrong.
18. *Il n'y a aucune difficulté.*	18. You're right.
19. *Il n'y a pas de quoi.*	19. I need that.
20. *Il y a longtemps.*	20. I'm twenty (years old).
21. *Il n'y a personne ici.*	21. Does he have any money?
22. *Venez aussi vite que possible.*	22. Does he have (any) friends in Paris?
23. *Y a-t-il des lettres pour moi?*	23. What's the matter with him?
24. *Il y a un jour.*	24. How old are you?
25. *Il n'y a pas de réponse.*	25. How many of them do you have?

ANSWERS

1—12; 2—16; 3—19; 4—17; 5—15; 6—13; 7—20; 8—14; 9—24; 10—21; 11—25; 12—22; 13—11; 14—18; 15—23; 16—8; 17—3; 18—4; 19—1; 20—9; 21—6; 22—10; 23—5; 24—7; 25—2.

LESSON 16

24. DO YOU SPEAK FRENCH?

(Do You Speak French?)

Vous parlez français?[1] / **Parlez-vous français?** / **Est-ce que vous parlez français?**	Do you speak French?
Non, je ne parle pas le français.	No, I don't speak French.
Je ne parle pas bien le français.	I don't speak French very well.
mal	poorly
très mal	very poorly
Je parle très mal.	I speak very poorly.
un peu	a little
Oui, je parle un peu.	Yes, I speak a little.
très peu	very little
Je parle très peu.	I speak very little.
Pas beaucoup.	Not much.
Quelques mots.	A few words.
Quelques mots seulement.	Only a few words.
Comprenez-vous?	Do you understand?
Non, je ne comprends pas.	No, I don't understand.
Je ne comprends pas bien.	I don't understand well.
Je ne comprends pas bien le français.	I don't understand French very well.
Oui, je comprends.	Yes, I understand.
Oui, je comprends un peu.	Yes, I understand a little.
Je lis mais je ne parle pas.	I read but I can't speak.

[1] Note: after the verb *parlez* the article *le* may be used or omitted.

Vous comprenez? **Comprenez-vous?** **Est-ce que vous comprenez?**	Do you understand?
Pas du tout.	Not at all.
Je comprends mal.	I don't know that word well.
Ecrivez-le.	Write it (down).
Comment l'écrivez-vous?	How do you write (spell) it?
Je ne connais pas ce mot.	I don't know that word.

25. PLEASE SPEAK MORE SLOWLY

Si vous parlez lentement je peux vous comprendre.	If you speak slowly I can understand you.
Si vous parlez lentement, je peux vous comprendre.	If you speak slowly, I'll be able to understand you.

LESSON 17

(Please Speak More Slowly)

Vous dites . . . ?	What did you say? ("You say . . . ?") (This is used where we would say: "You were saying?" "What was that?" "What did you say?" etc.)
Comment? Vous dites . . . ?	What did you say? ("How? You say . . . ?")

Comment dites-vous cela en français?	How do you say that in French?
Comment dit-on "Thank you" en français?	How do you say "Thank you" in French?
Que voulez-vous dire?	What do you mean? ("What do you want to say?")
voulez-vous . . . ?	would you . . . ?
parler	to speak
moins vite	slower ("less quickly")
Voulez-vous parler moins vite?	Would you speak slower?
s'il vous plaît	please.
Voulez-vous parler moins vite, s'il vous plaît?	Would you mind speaking a little slower, please?
je vous prie	please ("I beg you")
Voulez-vous parler moins vite, je vous prie?	Would you mind speaking a little slower, please?
Voulez-vous répéter, s'il vous plaît?	Would you please say that again?

26. THANKS

Parlez lentement, s'il vous plaît.	Please speak slowly.
Merci.	Thanks.
Je vous remercie.	Thanks. ("I thank you.")
Je vous en remercie.	Thanks. ("I thank you for it.")
Je vous remercie beaucoup.	Thank you very much.

Il n'y a pas de quoi.	Don't mention it.
Je vous remercie.	Thanks.
De rien.	Not at all.
Excusez-moi.	Excuse me.
De rien.	Certainly.
Vous permettez?	May I? ("You permit me?")
Faites! (Faites donc!)	Go ahead! Please do! ("Do!")
Je vous en prie.	Please do! ("I beg you.")
Pardon?	Pardon? What did you say?
Plaît-il?	What did you say? ("Will you please say that again?")
A bientôt.	See you soon. ("Until soon.")
A plus tard.	See you later. ("Until later.")
A ce soir.	See you this evening. ("Until this evening.")

QUIZ 7

1. *Ecrivez-le.*	1. No, I don't speak French.
2. *Non, je ne parle pas français.*	2. A few words.
3. *Je ne comprends pas bien le français.*	3. Do you understand?
4. *Comprenez-vous?*	4. I don't understand French very well.
5. *Quelques mots.*	5. Write (it) down.
6. *Voulez-vous rêpéter, s'il vous plaît?*	6. How do you write (spell) it?

7. *Comment dit-on "Thank you" en français?*	7. I don't know that word.
8. *Que voulez-vous dire?*	8. How do you say "Thank you" in French?
9. *Comment l'écrivez-vous?*	9. What do you mean? ("What do you want to say?")
10. *Je ne connais pas ce mot.*	10. Would you please say that again?

ANSWERS

1—5; 2—1; 3—4; 4—3; 5—2; 6—10; 7—8; 8—9; 9—6; 10—7.

WORD STUDY

le développement	development
la joie	joy
liquide	liquid
l'obligation (f.)	obligation
l'occupation (f.)	occupation
pâle	pale
populaire	popular
solide	solid
le théâtre	theatre
le voyage	voyage

27. THIS AND THAT

1. *ce* "this" or "that" *(masc.)*

ce matin	this (that) morning
ce soir	this evening; tonight
ce monsieur	this (that) gentleman

2. *cet* "this" or "that" *(before vowel or h)*

cet après-midi	this afternoon

cet argent	this (that) money
cet homme	this (that) man
cet hôtel	this (that) hotel

3. *cette* "this" or "that" *(fem.)*

cette femme	this (that) woman
cette historie	this (that) story
cette année	this (that) year

4. *ces* "these" or "those" *(masc.* and *fem.)*

ces messieurs	these (those) gentlemen
ces dames	these (those) ladies

5. *ce . . . -ci* "this"

ce livre-ci	this book
cet homme-ci	this man
cet hôtel-ci	this hotel
cette année-ci	this year
cette historie-ci	this story

6. *ce . . . -là* "that"

ce livre-là	that book
ce jour-là	that day
ce mot-là	that word
cet homme-là	that man
cet hôtel-là	that hotel
cette année-là	that year
cette historie-là	that story

7. *celui* "this one"

Je préfère celui-ci	I prefer this one *(masc.)*.
Je préfère celle-ci.	I prefer this one *(fem.)*.
Je préfère celui-là.	I prefer that one *(masc.)*
Je préfère celle-là.	I prefer that one *(fem.)*.
Je préfère ceux-ci.	I prefer these *(masc.* and *fem.)*.

Je préfère ceux-là.	I prefer those (*masc.* and *fem.*).

8. *ceci* "this"

Que veut dire ceci?	What does this mean?
Ceci est à moi.	This is mine.

9. *cela* "that"

C'est cela.	That's it. It's that.
Ne pensez pas à cela.	Don't think about that.
Cela va sans dire.	That goes without saying.
Ceci est à moi, cela est à vous.	This one is mine; that one is yours.

10. *ça* "that"

Ça is short for *cela* and has the same meaning. *Ça* is the form used in ordinary conversation; *cela* is more formal.

C'est ça.	It's that. That's it.
C'est bien ça.	That's quite right. Yes, that's right. I thought so.
Où ça?	Where? Where is that?
Ce n'est pas ça.	It isn't that. That's not it.
Ce n'est pas du tout ça.	It's not that at all.
Comme ça?	Like that?
Pas comme ça.	Not like that.
Donnez-moi ça.	Give me that.
Je n'aime pas ça.	I don't like that.
Ça m'est égal.	It's the same to me.
Ça me plait.	I like this (that).
Ça dépend.	That depends.
Ça va?	How are you? How are things?

Comment ça va?	How are things? Are things going well with you? Are you getting along all right?
Ça ne fait rien.	That doesn't matter. Never mind. Don't bother.

QUIZ 8

1. *Je préfère celui-là.*	1. What does this mean?
2. *Que veut dire ceci?*	2. This is mine.
3. *Donnez-moi ça.*	3. That goes without saying.
4. *Ça dépend.*	4. This one is mine, that one is yours.
5. *Ça m'est égal.*	5. It's not that at all.
6. *Ce n'est pas du tout ça.*	6. Give me that.
7. *Ça va?*	7. It's the same to me.
8. *Cela va sans dire.*	8. That depends.
9. *Ceci est à moi, cela est à vous.*	9. How are you? How are things?
10. *Ceci est à moi.*	10. I prefer that one (masc.).

ANSWERS

1—10; 2—1; 3—6; 4—8; 5—7; 6—5; 7—9; 8—3; 9—4; 10—2.

WORD STUDY

l'armée (f.)	army
la barrière	barrier
le caractère	character
curieux	curious

la curiosité	curiosity
le degré	degree
le dictionnaire	dictionary
l'officiel (m.)	official
ordinaire	ordinary
la pitié	pity

LESSON 18

28. NOT

(Useful Word Groups II)

Ce n'est pas bon.	It's not good.
Ce n'est pas mal.	It's not bad.
Ce n'est pas ça.	It's not that.
Ce n'est pas ici.	It's not here.
Pas trop.	Not too much.
Pas trop vite.	Not too fast.
Pas beaucoup.	Not much.
Pas assez.	Not enough.
Pas souvent.	Not often.
Pas encore.	Not yet.
Pas du tout.	Not at all.
Je n'ai pas de temps.	I haven't any time.
Je ne sais pas comment.	I don't know how.
Je ne sais pas quand.	I don't know when.
Je ne sais pas où.	I don't know where.
Je ne sais rien.	I don't know anything.
Il n'a rien dit.	He didn't say (hasn't said) anything.
Rien du tout.	Nothing.
Je n'ai rien.	I haven't anything.
Jamais.	Never.
Je ne le vois jamais.	I never see him.
Il ne vient jamais.	He never comes.

Qui est venu?—Personne.	Who came?—Nobody.
Je ne vois personne.	I don't see anyone.
Je n'y vais plus.	I don't go there any more.
Il ne vient plus.	He doesn't come any more.
Je n'ai que cent francs.	I have only a hundred francs.
Vous n'avez qu'une heure.	You have only one hour.
Il n'en a que dix.	He has only ten of them.

29. ISN'T IT?

N'est-ce pas?	Isn't it?
C'est vrai, n'est-ce pas?	It's true, isn't it?
Vous venez, n'est-ce pas?	You're coming, aren't you?
Vous en avez assez, n'est-ce pas?	You have enough of it, haven't you?
Vous n'en avez pas, n'est-ce pas?	You haven't any of it, have you?
Vous êtes d'accord, n'est-ce pas?	You agree, don't you?

QUIZ 9

1. Ce n'est pas ça.	1. I don't see anyone.
2. Je ne sais pas quand.	2. I have only a hundred francs.
3. Je n'ai pas de temps.	3. You have only one hour.
4. Rien du tout.	4. You're coming, aren't you?
5. Vous venez, n'est-ce-pas?	5. You haven't any of it, have you?

6. *Vous n'avez qu'une heure.*	6. It's not that.
7. *Je ne vois personne.*	7. I haven't any time.
8. *Je n'ai que cent francs.*	8. I don't know when.
9. *Vous n'en avez pas, n'est-ce pas?*	9. He didn't say (hasn't said) anything.
10. *Il n'a rien dit.*	10. Nothing.

ANSWERS

1—6; 2—8; 3—7; 4—10; 5—4; 6—3; 7—1; 8—2; 9—5; 10—9.

30. I, YOU, HIM

1. It's Me (I)

C'est moi.	It's me (I).
C'est toi.	It's you *(fam.)*.
C'est lui.	It's him (he).
C'est elle.	It's her (she).
C'est nous.	It's us (we).
C'est vous.	It's you.
C'est eux.	It's them (they) *(masc.)*.
C'est elles.	It's them (they) *(fem.)*

2. It's Mine.

C'est à moi.	It's mine.
C'est à toi.	It's yours *(fam.)*.
C'est à lui.	It's his.
C'est à elle.	It's hers.
C'est à nous.	It's ours.
C'est à vous.	It's yours *(pol.)*.
C'est à eux.	It's theirs *(masc.)*.
C'est à elles.	It's theirs *(fem.)*.

3. About Me

Je parle de toi.	I'm talking about you. *(fam.).*
Tu parles de moi.	You're talking about me.
Il parle de lui.	He's talking about him.
Elle parle de lui.	She's talking about him.
On parle d'elle.	People are talking about her.
Nous parlons de vous.	We're talking about you *(pol.).*
Vous parlez de nous.	You're talking about us.
Ils parlent d'eux.	They're talking about them *(masc.).*
Elles parlent d'elles.	They're talking about them *(fem.).*

4. To Me

Donnez-le moi.	Give it to me.
Donnez-le lui.	Give it to him (her).
Donnez-le nous	Give it to us.
Donnez-le leur.	Give it to them *(masc.* and *fem.).*
Donnez-ça.	Give it! Give this (that).
Donnez-moi ça.	Give it to me.
Donnez-lui ça.	Give it to him (her).
Donnez-nous ça.	Give it to us.
Donnez-leur ça.	Give it to them *(masc.* and *fem.).*

5. He Speaks to Me

Il me parle.	He speaks to me.
Il te parle.	He speaks to you.
Il lui parle.	He speaks to him (her).

Il nous parle.	He speaks to us.
Il vous parle.	He speaks to you.
Il leur parle.	He speaks to them (*masc.* and *fem.*).

6. He Gives It to Me

Il me le donne.	He gives it to me.
Il te le donne.	He gives it to you.
Il le lui donne.	He gives it to him (her).
Il nous le donne.	He gives it to us.
Il vous le donne.	He gives it to you.
Il le leur donne.	He gives it to them (*masc.* and *fem.*).

31. MINE, YOURS, HIS

SINGULAR

Masculine	*Feminine*	
le mien	*la mienne*	mine
le tien	*la tienne*	yours
le sien	*la sienne*	his, hers, its
le nôtre	*la nôtre*	ours
le vôtre	*la vôtre*	yours
le leur	*la leur*	theirs

PLURAL

les miens	*les miennes*	mine
les tiens	*les tiennes*	yours
les siens	*les siennes*	his, hers, its
les nôtres	*les nôtres*	ours
les vôtres	*les vôtres*	yours
les leurs	*les leurs*	theirs

C'est le mien.	It's mine.
C'est le nôtre.	It's ours.
C'est le leur.	It's theirs.
C'est la sienne.	It's his (hers).
Mes amis et les vôtres.	My friends and yours.
Votre livre est meilleur que le sien.	Your book is better than his.
Votre place est bonne, mais la leur est meilleure.	Your seat is good but theirs is better.
Quelle est la lettre qui est perdue?—C'est la sienne.	Which is the letter that was lost?—His.

32. MYSELF, YOURSELF, HIMSELF

1. I Wash Myself

Je me lave.	I wash myself.
Tu te laves.	You wash yourself.
Il se lave.	He washes himself.
Elle se lave.	She washes herself.
On se lave.	One washes oneself.
Nous nous lavons.	We wash ourselves.
Vous vous laves.	You wash yourselves.
Ils se lavent.	They wash themselves (*masc.*).
Elles se lavent.	They wash themselves (*fem.*).

Notice that myself, yourself, etc. is *me, te,*etc. Verbs that take *me, te,* etc. are called "reflexive verbs." Many verbs that do not take "myself," "yourself,", etc. in English do so in French:

Je me lève.	I get up. ("I raise myself.")
Je me rappelle.	I recall.
Je me sers.	I use.

Je m'arrête.	I stop.
Je me trompe.	I'm mistaken. I'm wrong.
Je me tourne.	I turn around.
Je m'amuse.	I'm having a good time.
Je m'ennuie.	I'm bored.

Other Examples:

Il se peigne.	He's combing himself.
Je me suis acheté un chapeau.	I bought myself a hat.
Où se lave-t-on les mains?	Where can one wash his hands?
Je me sers de ça.	I'm using that.

WORD STUDY

absolu	absolute
l'aspect (m.)	aspect
la barre	bar
certain	certain
la combinaison	combination
le danger	danger
l'échange (m.)	exchange
la manière	manner
le reproche	reproach
le total	total

QUIZ 10

1. *Donnez-leur ça.*	1. I'm using that.
2. *Il parle de lui.*	2. I bought myself a hat.
3. *Ils parlent d'eux.*	3. My friends and yours.
4. *Il le leur donne.*	4. He washes himself.
5. *Mes amis et les vôtres.*	5. I recall.

6. *Je m'amuse.*
7. *Je me rappelle.*
8. *Je me suis acheté un chapeau.*
9. *Il se lave.*
10. *Je me sers de ça.*

6. He gives it to them (*masc.* and *fem.*).
7. I'm having a good time.
8. He's talking about him.
9. Give it to them (*masc.* and *fem.*).
10. They're talking about them.

ANSWERS

1—9; 2—8; 3—10; 4—6; 5—3; 6—7; 7—5; 8—2; 9—4; 10—1.

LESSON 19

33. HELLO!

(Hello! How Are Things?)

Bonjour.
Hello. Good Morning. Good afternoon.

Bonjour, Monsieur Dupont.
Hello, Mr. Dupont. Good morning (afternoon), Mr. Dupont.

Comment allez-vous?
How are you? How do you do?

{**Je vais bien, merci.**
{**Tres bien, merci.**

Very well, thanks.

Comment allez-vous? is the formal way of saying "How are you?" The more familiar way is: *Comment ça va? or Ça va?*

Comment ça va?
How are you? How are things? ("How does it go?")

Très bien, merci.
Very well, thanks.

Comme ci, comme ça.
So, so.

Et vous?
And how are you? ("And you?")

Pas mal.
Not too bad.

Pas mal, merci.
Not too bad, thanks.

Pas mal du tout.
Not too bad. ("Not bad at all.")

Ça va?
How are you? How are things? ("It goes?")

Oui, ça va.
All right. Fine. ("Yes, it goes.")

Oui, ça va bien.
All right. Fine. ("Yes, it goes well.")

34. I'D LIKE YOU TO MEET . . .

Permettez-moi de vous présenter Madame Dupont.
Allow me to present ("to you") Mrs. Dupont.

Permettez-moi de vous présenter Monsieur Dupont.
Allow me to present ("to you") Mr. Dupont.

Je suis heureux de faire votre connaissance.
Glad to know you. Glad to meet you.

Je suis heureux de faire votre connaissance, Madame.
Glad to know you (madam). Glad to meet you (madam).

Et voici Monsieur Dupont.
This is Mr. Dupont. ("And here is . . .")

Très heureux, Monsieur.[1]
Glad to know you.

35. HOW ARE THINGS?

Bonjour!
Hello!

Ça va?
How are you? How are things? ("It goes?").

Ça va bien, merci.
Fine, thanks.

Et vous?
How are you? ("And you?").

Comme ci, comme ça.
So, so.

Alors, quelles nouvelles?
Well, what's new?

Quoi de neuf?
What's new?

Rien de neuf.
Rien de nouveau.
Nothing much. ("Nothing new.")

Téléphonez-moi un de ces jours.
Phone me one of these days.

N'y manquez pas.
Don't forget. ("Don't fail.")

[1] A very colloquial expression for "Glad to know you" is *Enchanté: Et voici Monsieur Dupont.—Enchanté, Monsieur.* "This is Mr. Dupont.—Glad to know you."

Je n'y manquerai pas.
I'll do so without fail. ("I won't fail.")

Bien vrai?
You're sure? ("True? Really?")

Bien vrai!
Sure! ("True! Really!")

A la prochaine fois.
See you soon. ("Until the next time.")

A bientôt.
See you soon.

A tout à l'heure.
See you soon. See you in a little while.

A lundi.
Till Monday. See you Monday.

A demain.
Till tomorrow. See you tomorrow.

Je vous verrai dans huit jours.
I'll see you in a week ("in eight days").

Je vous verrai dans quinze jours.
I'll see you in two weeks ("in fifteen days").

Je vous verrai vendredi soir.
I'll see you Friday evening.

Je vous verrai jeudi prochain.
I'll see you next Thursday.

Je vous verrai jeudi prochain à huit heures du soir.
I'll see you next Thursday at eight o'clock (in the evening).

Je vous verrai ce soir.
I'll see you this evening (tonight).

QUIZ 11

1. *Ça va?*
2. *Comme ci, comme ça.*
3. *Je suis heureux de faire votre connaissance.*
4. *Quoi de neuf?*
5. *Alors, quelles nouvelles?*
6. *Je vais bien, merci.*
7. *Rien de nouveau.*
8. *Bonjour.*
9. *Pas mal du tout.*
10. *Comment allez-vous?*
11. *A tout à l'heure.*
12. *Téléphonez-moi un de ces jours.*
13. *A la prochaine fois.*
14. *Permettez-moi . . .*
15. *A lundi.*

1. How are you? How do you do?
2. Very well, thanks.
3. Not too bad. ("Not bad at all.")
4. How are you? How are things? ("It goes?")
5. So, so.
6. I'm happy to know you.
7. What's new?
8. Well, what's new?
9. Good morning. Good afternoon. Hello.
10. Nothing much. ("Nothing new.")
11. Allow me . . .
12. Phone me one of these days.
13. See you Monday. ("Until Monday.")
14. See you soon.(Until the next time.")
15. See you soon. See you in a little while.

ANSWERS

1—4; 2—5; 3—6; 4—7; 5—8; 6—2; 7—10; 8—9; 9—3; 10—1; 11—15; 12—12; 13—14; 14—11; 15—13.

LESSON 20

36. HAVE YOU TWO MET?

(Have You Two Met?)

Est-ce que vous connaissez mon ami?
Do you know my friend?

Non, je ne pense pas.
No, I don't think so.

Non, je n'ai pas ce plaisir.
No, I haven't had the pleasure.

Vous vous connaissez déjà, je crois?
I believe you already know one another.

Oui, nous nous sommes déjà rencontrés.
Yes, we've already met.

Non, je ne connais pas monsieur.
No, I don't believe we've met before. ("No, I don't know the gentleman.")

J'ai déjà eu [1] le plaisir de rencontrer monsieur.
I've already had the pleasure of meeting him ("of meeting the gentleman.")

[1] *eu* (pronounced as though written *u*) is a form of *avoir: j'ai eu* "I have had."

37. GLAD TO HAVE MET YOU

Enchanté d'avoir fait votre connaissance.
Enchanté de vous avoir rencontré.
Glad to have met you.

J'espère vous revoir bientôt.
Hope to see you soon.

Moi aussi.
The same here.

Retrouvons-nous un de ces jours!
Let's get together again one of these days.

C'est ça.
Fine. ("That's it.")

Vous avez mon adresse et mon téléphone?
Do you have my address and telephone number?

Non, donnez-les moi.
No, let me have them. ("Give them to me.")

Mon adresse est quinze (15) Avenue de la Grande Armée.
My address is 15 Grand Armée Avenue.

Mon numéro de téléphone est Etoile cinquante-quatre, cinquante-deux (54-52).
My telephone number is Etoile 5452.

Donnez-moi aussi l'adresse de votre bureau.
Give me your office address also.

Je vais[1] vous l'écrire; c'est au cent deux (102) Avenue des Champs-Elysées.
I'll write it for you. It's 102 Champs-Elysées Avenue.

Vous pouvez m'appeler à la maison le matin avant neuf heures.
You can get me at home before nine in the morning.

[1] *Je vais* "I'm going" is from *aller* "to go" (see page 117).

Ensuite, au bureau.
Otherwise ("afterwards") at the office.

Entendu, je n'y manquerai pas.
Good, I'll do that. ("Understood, I won't fail to do so.")

Au revoir et n'oubliez pas de me donner un coup de fil.
Good-by and don't forget to give me a ring.

Non, je n'oublierai pas. A bientôt.
No, I won't forget. See you soon.

QUIZ 12

1. *Non, je ne pense pas.*
2. *Oui, nous nous sommes déjà rencontrés.*
3. *Non, donnez-les moi.*
4. *Donnez-moi aussi l'adresse de votre bureau.*
5. *A bientôt.*
6. *Entendu, je n'y manquerai pas.*
7. *Vous avez mon adresse et mon téléphone?*
8. *Non, je n'ai pas ce plaisir.*
9. *J'espère vous revoir bientôt.*
10. *Enchanté d'avoir fait votre connaissance.*

1. Yes, we've already met.
2. No, I haven't had the pleasure.
3. No, I don't think so.
4. Glad to have met you.
5. (I) hope to see you soon.
6. Give me your officc addrcss also.
7. No, let me have them. ("Give them to me.")
8. Do you have my address and telephone number?
9. Good, I'll do that. ("Understood, I won't fail to do so.")
10. Good-by. ("See you soon.")

ANSWERS

1—3; 2—1; 3—7; 4—6; 5—10; 6—9; 7—8; 8—2; 9—5; 10—4.

WORD STUDY

le collège	college
la conclusion	conclusion
la condition	condition
la considération	consideration
la décision	decision
la personne	person
la saison	season
la scène	scene
le signal	signal

REVIEW QUIZ 2

1. *Voulez-vous*—(speak) *moins vite, s'il vous plaît.*
   a. *dire*
   b. *parler*
   c. *répéter*

2. *Parlez plus*—(slowly), *s'il vous plaît.*
   a. *vite*
   b. *moins*
   c. *lentement*

3. *Je donne*—(the) *livre à l'enfant.*
   a. *un*
   b. *le*
   c. *la*

4. *Il donne*—(a) *lettre à une femme.*
   a. *une*
   b. *la*
   c. *les*

5. *Ce n'est pas bien*—(far).
   a. loin
   b. ici
   c. là

6. *Il donne de l'argent*—(to the) *pauvres.*
   a. à
   b. aux
   c. je

7. *Je*—(am) *dans la chambre.*
   a. a
   b. suis
   c. pas

8. *Il n'est pas*—(late).
   a. suis
   b. vous
   c. tard

9. *Où*—(are) *vos livres?*
   a. ses
   b. sont
   c. est

10. —(bring) *moi un verre.*
    a. voudrais
    b. donnez
    c. apportez

11. *C'est*—(less) *difficile.*
    a. moins
    b. plus
    c. rien

12. *C'est*—(for) *les enfants.*
    a. vous
    b. our
    c. par

13. *Je n'*—(have) *pas d'argent.*
 a. ai
 b. ont
 c. rien

14. *Est-ce que vous*—(have) *des cigarettes?*
 a. a
 b. avons
 c. avez

15. *Je ne*— (understand) *pas bien le français.*
 a. comprends
 b. parle
 c. plaît

16. *Je vous en*—(thank) *beaucoup.*
 a. lentement
 b. remercie
 c. comprends

17. *Est-il*—(here)*?*
 a. où
 b. que
 c. ici

18. *Est-ce qu'ils son?*—(ready)*?*
 a. vrai
 b. prêts
 c. ici

19. *Est-ce ue c'est*—(true)*?*
 a. prêt
 b. vrai
 c. où

20. *Je comprends un*—(little).
 a. seulement
 b. très
 c. peu

ANSWERS

1—b.; 2—c.; 3—b.; 4—b.; 5—a.; 6—b.; 7—b.; 8—c.; 9—b.; 10—c.; 11—a.; 12—b.; 13—a.; 14—c.; 15—a.; 16—b.; 17—c.; 18—b.; 19—b.; 20—c.

LESSON 21

38. NUMBERS

(Numbers 1)

1. One, Two, Three

un (une)	one
deux	two
trois	three
quatre	four
cinq	five
six	six
sept	seven
huit	eight
neuf	nine
dix	ten
onze	eleven
douze	twelve
treize	thirteen
quatorze	fourteen
quinze	fifteen
seize	sixteen
dix-sept	seventeen
dix-huit	eighteen
dix-neuf	nineteen

vingt	twenty
vingt et un	twenty-one
vingt-deux	twenty-two
vingt-trois	twenty-three
trente	thirty
trente et un	thirty-one
trente-deux	thirty-two
trente-trois	thirty-three
quarante	forty
quarante et un	forty-one
quarante-deux	forty-two
quarante-trois	forty-three
cinquante	fifty
cinquante et un	fifty-one
cinquante-deux	fifty-two
cinquante-trois	fifty-three
soixante	sixty
soixante et un	sixty-one
soixante-deux	sixty-two
soixante-trois	sixty-three
soixante-dix	seventy
soixante et onze	seventy-one
soixante-douze	seventy-two
soixante-treize	seventy-three
quatre-vingts	eighty
quatre-vingt-un	eighty-one
quatre-vingt-deux	eighty-two
quatre-vingt-trois	eighty-three
quatre-vingt-dix	ninety
quatre-vingt-onze	ninety-one
quatre-vingt-douze	ninety-two
quatre-vingt-treize	ninety-three

cent	hundred
cent un	a hundred and one
cent deux	a hundred and two
cent trois	a hundred and three

mille[1]	thousand
mille un	a thousand one
millc deux	a thousand and two
mille trois	a thousand and three

2. Some More Numbers

cent vingt	a hundred and twenty
cent vingt-deux	a hundred and twenty-two
cent trente	a hundred and thirty
cent quarante	a hundred and forty
cent cinquante	a hundred and fifty
cent soixante	a hundred and sixty
cent soixante-dix	a hundred and seventy
cent soixante et onze	a hundred and seventy-one
cent soixante-dix-huit	a hundred and seventy-eight
cent quatre-vingt	a hundred and eighty
cent quatre-vingt-deux	a hundred and eighty-two
cent quatre-vingt-dix	a hundred and ninety
cent quatre-vingt-dix-huit	a hundred and ninety-eight
cent quatre-vingt-dix-neuf	a hundred and ninety-nine
deux cents	two hundred
trois cent vingt-quatre	three hundred and twenty-four

[1] *Mille* used to be written *mil* in dates: *mil neuf cent douz* —1912.

It frequently appears this way on monuments.

huit cent soixante-quinze	eight hundred and seventy-five

LESSON 22

(Numbers II)

The pronunciation of the numbers often differs before words beginning with a vowel or *h*. Compare the following columns—the first containing nouns beginning with a consonant; the second, nouns beginning with a vowel or *h*:

	BEGINNING WITH A CONSONANT	BEGINNING WITH A VOWEL OR H
1.	**un fils** a son	**un homme** a man
2.	**deux jeunes filles** two young girls	**deux heures** two hours
3.	**trois jours** three days	**trois enfants** three children
4.	**quatre garçons** four boys	**quatre étages** four floors
5.	**cinq mètres** five meters	**cinq ans** five years
6.	**six kilomètres** six kilometers	**six autres** six others
7.	**sept chiens** seven dogs	**sept hôtels** seven hotels
8.	**huit semaines** eight weeks	**huit heures** eight hours
9.	**neuf mois** nine months	**neuf ans** nine years

10.	**dix leçons** ten lessons	**dix ans** ten years
11.	**vingt minutes** twenty minutes	**vingt hommes** twenty men
12.	**cent francs** a hundred francs	**cent ans** a hundred years

3. First, Second, Third

1. **premier (première)**	first
2. **deuxième**	second
3. **troisième**	third
4. **quatrième**	fourth
5. **cinquième**	fifth
6. **sixième**	sixth
7. **septième**	seventh
8. **huitième**	eighth
9. **neuvième**	ninth
10. **dixième**	tenth

le premier livre	the first book
la première chose	the first thing
le deuxième acte or *le second acte*	the second act
la troisième classe	the third class
le quatrième étage	the fourth floor
la cinquième leçon	the fifth lesson
le sixième jour	the sixth day
la septième semaine	the seventh week
le huitième mois	the eighth month
la neuvième année	the ninth year
la dixième lettre	the tenth letter
la onzième personne	the eleventh person
le douzième chapitre	the twelfth chapter
le treizième invité	the thirteenth guest

le quatorzième paquet	the fourteenth package
la quinzième porte	the fifteenth door
le seizième bateau	the sixteenth boat
la dix-septième rue	the seventeenth street
la dix-huitième édition	the eighteenth edition
la dix-neuvième auto	the nineteenth car
la vingtième maison	the twentieth house

QUIZ 13

1. six kilomètres	1. the third class
2. deux jeunes filles	2. the eighth month
3. vingt minutes	3. the ninth year
4. la troisième classe	4. six kilometers
5. dix-neuvième	5. two young girls
6. la onzième personne	6. twenty minutes
7. dix-septième	7. the eleventh person
8. le huitième mois	8. thirteenth
9. treizième	9. seventeenth
10. la neuvième année	10. nineteenth

ANSWERS

1—4; 2—5; 3—6; 4—1; 5—10; 6—7; 7—9; 8—2; 9—8; 10—3.

4. Two and Two

Deux et un font trois.
Two and one are three.

Ou- or

Deux plus un font trois.
Two and ("plus") one are three.

Deux et deux font quatre.
Two and two are four.

Ou- or

Deux plus deux font quatre.
Two and ("plus") two are four.

Quatre et trois font sept.
Four and three are seven.

Ou- or

Quatre plus trois font sept.
Four and ("plus") three are seven.

Cinq et deux font sept.
Five and two are seven.

Ou- or

Cinq plus deux font sept.
Five and ("plus") two are seven.

Sept et un font huit.
Seven and one are eight.

Ou- or

Sept plus un font huit.
Seven and ("plus") one are eight.

LESSON 23

39. IT COSTS . . .

(Numbers III)

Ceci coûte . . .
This costs . . .

Ceci coûte cinq francs.
This costs five francs.

Ce livre coûte dix francs cinquante.
This book costs ten franc fifty centimes.

Ce chapeau m'a coûté cinquante-quatre francs.
This hat cost me fifty-four francs.

J'ai payé deux cents francs pour cette robe.
I paid two hundred francs for this dress.

J'ai acheté cette voiture pour dix mille francs.
I bought this car for ten thousand francs.

C'est deux francs le litre.
It's two francs a liter.

Cela coûte vingt-cinq francs le mètre.
That costs twenty-five francs a meter.

Son prix est de douze cents francs.
The price is twelve hundred francs.
It costs twelve hundred francs.

Ils coûtent cinquante centimes pièce.
They cost fifty centimes apiece.

40. THE TELEPHONE NUMBER IS . . .

Mon numéro de téléphone est Central trente-six, quarante-deux.[1]
My telephone number is Central 3642.

Essayez donc le numéro Trudaine cinquante-deux, trente-six.
Try number Trudaine 5236.

Mon numéro de téléphone a été changé: c'est maintenant Opéra vingt-deux, vingt-quatre.
My telephone number has been changed: it's now Opera 2224.

[1] Notice how French telephone numbers differ from ours: Central 3642 is not three, six, four, two as in English but thirty-six, forty-two.

Leur numéro de téléphone est Littré trente-trois, zéro sept.
Their phone number is Littré 3307.

41. THE NUMBER IS . . .

J'habite au numéro dix-sept de la rue Balzac.
I live at 17 Balzac Street

Il habite au numéro quatre du Boulevard Haussmann.
He lives at 4 Haussmann Boulevard.

Notre adresse est onze, rue de Nice.
Our address is 11 Nice Street.

Nous habitons au numéro deux cent soixante-trois Avenue de Versailles.
We live at 263 Versailles Avenue.

Le numéro de ma chambre est quarante-deux.
My room number is 42.

42. SOME DATES

L'Amérique fut découverte en mil quatre cent quatre-vingt-douze (ou en quatorze cent quatre-vingt-douze).
America was discovered in 1492.

Cela s'est passé en mil huit cent quatre-vingt-onze (ou en dix-huit-cent quatre-vingt-onze).
It happened in 1891.

Je suis né en mil neuf cent douze (or en dix-neuf cent douze).
I was born in 1912.

Tout cela s'est passé en dix-neuf cent vingt-quatre (or *mil neuf cent vingt-quatre).*
All this happened in 1924.

L'exposition internationale de Paris eut lieu en mil neuf cent trente-sept (or *dix-neuf cent trente-sept.)*
The Paris World's Fair took place in 1937.

J'étais à Paris en mil neuf cent quarante (or *dix-neuf cent quarante).*
I was in Paris in 1940.

WORD STUDY

l'avance (f.)	advance
la banque	bank
le chapitre	chapter
content	content
délicieux	delicious
l' ennemi (m.)	enemy
le fruit	fruit
le million	million
le péril	peril
riche	rich

QUIZ 14

1. *Ceci coûte cinq francs.*
2. *Leur numéro de téléphone est Littré trente-trois, zéro sept.*
3. *J'ai acheté cette voiture pour dix mille francs.*
4. *J'étais à Paris en mil neuf cent quarante* (or *dix neuf cent quarante).*
5. *Ils coûtent cinquante centimes pièce.*

1. This costs five francs.
2. I bought this car for ten thousand francs.
3. Their phone number is Littré 3307.
4. They cost fifty centimes each.
5. I was in Paris in 1940.

ANSWERS

1—1; 2—3; 3—2; 4—5; 5—4.

PARIS, SOUS L'OCCUPATION
(PARIS DURING THE OCCUPATION)

Un étudiant: "Taxi, vous êtes libre?"
A student: "Taxi, are you free?"

Le taxi s'arrête près du trottoir et attend le client.
The taxi pulls up to the curb and waits for the customer.

L'étudiant: "Vive la liberté!" et il continue à marcher.
The student: "Long live freedom!" and he walks away.

NOTES

Sous under

Vive la liberté! Long live freedom!

S'arrêter près du trottoir to stop near the sidewalk

Il continue à he continues to

LESSON 24

43. WHAT TIME IS IT?

(What Time Is It?)

Quelle heure est-il?
What time is it?

Avez-vous l'heure, s'il vous plaît?
Do you have the time, please?

Il est une heure.
It's one o'clock.

Il est deux heures.
It's two o'clock.

Il est trois heures.
It's three o'clock.

Il est quatre heures.
It's four o'clock.

Il est cinq heures.
It's five o'clock.

Il est six heures.
It's six o'clock.

Il est sept heures.
It's seven o'clock.

Il est huit heures.
It's eight o'clock.

Il est neuf heures.
It's nine o'clock.

Il est dix heures.
It's ten o'clock.

Il est onze heures.
It's eleven o'clock.

Il est midi.
It's noon. It's twelve o'clock.

Il est treize heures.
It's one p.m. ("thirteen o'clock").

Il est quatorze heures.
It's two p.m. ("fourteen o'clock").

Il est quinze heures.
It's three p.m ("fifteen o'clock").

Il est seize heures.
It's four p.m. ("sixteen o'clock").

Il est dix-sept heures.
It's five p.m. ("seventeen o'clock").

Il est dix-huit heures.
It's six p.m. ("eighteen o'clock").

Il est dix-neuf heures.
It's seven p.m. ("nineteen o'clock").

Il est vingt heures.
It's eight p.m. ("twenty o'clock").

Il est vingt-et-une heures.
It's nine p.m. ("twenty-one o'clock").

Il est vingt-deux heures.
It's ten p.m. ("twenty-two o'clock").

Il est vingt-trois heures.
It's eleven p.m. ("twenty-three o'clock").

Il est vingt-quatre heures.
It's twelve p.m. ("twenty-four o'clock").

Il est minuit.
It's midnight.

When you want to specify whether you mean "seven a.m." or "p.m." you say *sept heures du martin* ("seven hours of the morning") or *sept heures du soir* ("seven hours of the evening"). Official time (formal announcements of meetings, timetables, etc.) is on a twenty-four hour basis, like our Army time. Thus in a formal announcement you may see *dix-sept heures et demie for* 5:30 p.m. Ordinarily, however, you say *cinq heures et demie de l'après-midi*—that is, instead of our "a.m." and "p.m." you add when necessary *du matin, de l'après-midi* or *du soir*.

44. THE TIME IS NOW . . .

seconde	second
minute	minute
heure	hour

Il est deux heures quinze.
It's two fifteen.

Il est deux heures et quart.
It's a quarter after two.

Il est quatre heures moins le quart.
Il est quatre heures moins un quart.
It's a quarter to four.

Il est trois heures quarante-cinq.
It's three forty-five.

Il est deux heures et demie.
It's half past two.

Il est deux heures trente.
It's two thirty.

Il est cinq heures moins vingt.
It's twenty to five.

Il est neuf heures trente-cinq.
Its nine thirty-five.

Il est midi.
It's noon.

Il est midi moins cinq.
It's five to twelve.

Il est midi cinq.
It's five past twelve.

Il est une heure du matin.
It's one o'clock in the morning.

Il est à peu près cinq heures.
It's about five.

Il est près de sept heures.
It's about seven.

Il est presque onze heures.
It's almost eleven.

Il n'est que six heures et demie.
It's only half past six.

Il est plus de cinq heures.
It's after five.

45. A MATTER OF TIME

A quelle heure viendrez-vous?
When will you come? What time will you come?

Je serai là à trois heures.
I'll be there (at) three o'clock.

Elle est venue à trois heures moins vingt.
She came at twenty to three.

Il viendra à deux heures de l'après-midi.
He'll come at two p.m.

Nous serons là vers neuf heures vingt-cinq.
We'll be there about nine twenty-five.

Il reviendra à dix heures et demie du soir.
He'll be back (at) ten thirty tonight.

Je vous verrai là vers huit heures et quart.
I'll see you there about (''toward'') eight fifteen.

Nous nous verrons à six heures.
We'll meet (''see each other'') at six.

Je sors à quatre heures.
I'm going out (at) four o'clock.

Venez entre sept et huit.
Come between seven and eight.

Il viendra à six heures du soir.
He'll come (at) six in the evening.

Venez vers dix heures ce soir.
Come (at) ten o'clock tonight.

Le train arrive à sept heures vingt-trois.
The train arrives at seven twenty-three.

Le train part à neuf heures quarante.
The train leaves at nine forty.

WORD STUDY

l'angle (m.)	angle
la cause	cause
la conviction	conviction
la distance	distance
l'effet (m.)	effect
l'instant (m.)	instant
obscur	obscure
le propriétaire	proprietor
la qualité	quality
la quantité	quantity

QUIZ 15

1. *Il est deux heures et demie.*
2. *Il est deux heures quinze. Il est deux heures et quart.*
3. *Il est neuf heures trente-cinq.*
4. *Venez entre sept et huit.*
5. *Je vous verrai là vers huit heures et quart.*
6. *Le train arrive à sept heures vingt-trois.*
7. *Venez vers dix heures ce soir.*
8. *Il est une heure du matin.*
9. *Nous serons là vers neuf heures vingt-cinq.*
10. *Il viendra à deux heures de l'après-midi.*

1. I'll see you there about eight fifteen.
2. The train arrives at seven twenty-three.
3. Come between seven and eight.
4. Come at ten o'clock tonight.
5. It's one o'clock in the morning.
6. He'll come at two p.m.
7. We'll be there about nine twenty-five.
8. It's two fifteen. It's a quarter after two.
9. It's half past two. It's two thirty.
10. It's nine thirty-five.

ANSWERS

1—9; 2—8; 3—10; 4—3; 5—1; 6—2; 7—4; 8—5; 9—7; 10—6.

LESSON 25

46. IT'S TIME

(It's One O'Clock)

Il est temps.
It's time.

Il est temps de le faire.
It's time to do it.

Il est temps de partir.
It's time to leave.

Il est temps de rentrer.
It's time to go home.

J'ai le temps.
I have time.

Jai assez de temps.
I have enough time.

Je n'ai pas le temps.
I haven't the time.

Combien de temps avez-vous l'intention de rester ici?
How long do you intend to stay here?

Depuis combien de temps êtes-vous ici?
Depuis quand êtes-vous ici?
How long have you been here?

Il perd son temps.
He's wasting his time.

Donnez-lui le temps de le faire.
Give him time to do it.

Donnez-moi le temps de m'habiller.
Just give me enough time to get dressed.

Il vient de temps en temps.
He comes from time to time.

47. MORNING, NOON AND NIGHT

le matin	morning
le midi	noon
l'après-midi	afternoon
le soir	evening
la nuit	night
le jour	the day
la semaine	the week
huit jours	a week ("eight days")
quinze jours	two weeks ("fifteen days")
le mois	month
l'année	year
hier	yesterday
aujourd'hui	today
demain	tomorrow
avant-hier	the day before yesterday
le lendemain	the next day
après-demain	the day after tomorrow

il y a un moment	a moment ago
maintenant	now
dans un moment	in a moment
il y a longtemps	a long time ago
il y a peu de temps	a little while ago
ce matin	this morning
hier matin	yesterday morning
demain matin	tomorrow morning
cet après-midi	this afternoon
hier après-midi	yesterday afternoon
demain après-midi	tomorrow afternoon
ce soir	this evening
hier soir	yesterday evening
demain soir	tomorrow evening
cette nuit	tonight
la nuit passée	last night
la nuit prochaine	tomorrow night

LESSON 26

(Morning, Noon and Night)

cette semaine
cette semaine-ci
this week

la semaine passée
la semaine dernière
last week

la semaine prochaine
next week

dans deux semaines
in two weeks, the week after next

il y a deux semaines
two weeks ago, the week before last

{**ce mois**
{**ce mois-ci**
this month

{**le mois passé**
{**le mois dernier**
last month

le mois prochain
next month

dans deux mois
in two months, the month after next

il y a deux mois
two months ago, the month before last

cette année
this year

l'année dernière
last year

{**l'année prochaine**
{**l'an prochain**
next year

dans deux ans
in two years, the year after next

il y a deux ans
two years ago, the year before last

dans la matinée
in the moring

dans la soirée
in the evening

vers l'heure du déjeuner
toward lunch time

vers l'heure du dîner
toward dinner time

après-dîner
after dinner

à la fin de la semaine
at the end of the week

à la fin du mois
at the end of the month

vers la fin de la semaine
toward the end of the week

il y a une heure
an hour ago

dans un quart d'heure
in a quarter of an hour

un de ces jours
one of these days

A l'un de ces jours.
See you one of these days.

tous les jours
every day

toute la journée
all day (long)

toute la nuit
all night (long)

Il travaille du matin au soir.
He works from morning to night.

Quel jour du mois est-ce aujourd'hui?
What's the date? ("What day of the month is it today?")

48. PAST, PRESENT AND FUTURE

PASSÉ

il y a un instant
a moment ago
hier matin
yesterday morning
hier après-midi
yesterday afternoon
hier soir
yesterday evening, last night

la semain dernière
last week
le mois dernier
last month
l'année dernière
last year

PRÉSENT

maintenant
now
ce matin
this morning
cet après-midi
this afternoon
ce soir
this evening, tonight

cette semaine
this week
ce mois-ci
this month
cette année
this year

FUTUR

dans un instant
in a moment
demain matin
tomorrow morning
demain après-midi
tomorrow afternoon
demain soir
tomorrow-evening, tomorrow night

la semaine prochaine
next week
le mois prochain
next month
l'année prochaine
next year

LESSON 27

49. THE DAYS OF THE WEEK

(What's the Date?)

(Les jours de la semaine)

lundi	Monday
mardi	Tuesday
mercredi	Wednesday
jeudi	Thursday
vendredi	Friday
samedi	Saturday
dimanche	Sunday

50. WHAT'S THE DATE TODAY?

The following expressions are all used for "What's the date today?"

Quel jour sommes-nous?
"What day are we?"

Quel jour sommes-nous aujourd'hui?
"What day are we today?"

Nous sommes le combien?
"We are the how many?"

Le combien sommes-nous?
"The how many are we?"

Le combien est-ce?
"The how many is it?"

Samedi est le combien?
What's the date Saturday?

Nous sommes le dix.
Today's the tenth. ("We are the tenth.")

Nous sommes le vingt.
Today's the twentieth.

Sommes-nous mardi ou mercredi?
Is today Tuesday or Wednesday? ("Are we Tuesday or Wednesday?")

Nous sommes aujourd'hui mercredi.
Today's Wednesday.

C'est aujourd'hui lundi.
Today's Monday.

Venez samedi prochain.
Come next Saturday.

Il partira mardi prochain.
He'll leave next Tuesday. He's leaving next Tuesday.

Il est arrivé lundi dernier.
He arrived last Monday.

Il arrivera lundi prochain.
He'll arrive next Monday. He's arriving next Monday.

QUIZ 16

1. *avant-hier*
2. *aujourd'hui*
3. *l'après-midi*
4. *il y a un instant*
5. *demain après-midi*
6. *cet après-midi*
7. *après-demain*
8. *Il perd son temps.*
9. *toute la nuit*
10. *Depuis combien de temps êtes-vous ici?*
11. *la semaine prochaine*

12. *la semaine dernière*
13. *il y a deux semaines*
14. *dans deux mois*
15. *il y a deux ans*
16. *Il est temps.*
17. *J'ai le temps.*
18. *Il est temps de rentrer.*
19. *demain soir*
20. *ce soir*

1. afternoon
2. day before yesterday
3. today
4. day after tomorrow
5. a moment ago
6. tomorrow afternoon
7. all night (long)
8. He's wasting his time.
9. this afternoon
10. How long have you been here?
11. in two months, the month after next
12. two weeks ago, the week before last
13. next week
14. two years ago, the year before last
15. last week
16. It's time to go home.
17. tomorrow night
18. tonight
19. It's time.
20. I have time.

ANSWERS

1—2; 2—3; 3—1; 4—5; 5—6; 6—9; 7—4; 8—8; 9—7; ; 10—10; 11—13; 12—15; 13—12; 14—11; 15—14; 16—19; 17—20; 18—16; 19—17; 20—18.

51. THE MONTHS

(Les mois de l'année)

janvier	January
février	February
mars	March
avril	April
mai	May
juin	June
juillet	July
août	August
septembre	September
octobre	October
novembre	November
décembre	December

C'est aujourd'hui le premier juin.
Today is the first of June.

Je suis né le douze avril.
I was born (on) April 12th.

Ma soeur est née le cinq mai.
My sister was born (on) May 5th.

Mon anniversaire est le deux février.
My birthday is February 2nd.

Je viendrai le quatorze juillet.
I'll come (on) the 14th of July.

L'école commence le vingt septembre.
School begins (on) the 20th of September.

Je reviendrai le vingt-deux mars.
I'll be back (on) March 22nd.

Le onze novembre est un jour de congé.
November 11th is a holiday.

Il partira le six juillet.
He's leaving (on) July 6th.

La lettre est datée du six juin.
The letter is dated June 6th.

Nous viendrons vous voir le onze mai.
We'll come to see you (on) May 11th.

Nous sommes le deux mai dix-neuf cent quarante-cinq (or **mil neuf cent quarante-cinq**).
Today is May 2nd, 1945.

52. THE SEASONS

(Les saisons)

le printemps	spring
l'été	summer
l'automne	autumn
l'hiver	winter
en hiver	in winter
en été	in summer
en automne	in autumn, in the fall
au printemps	in spring

QUIZ 17

1. *Quel jour sommes-nous?*
2. *A l'un de ces jours.*
3. *toute la journée*
4. *on été*
5. *dans un quart d'heure*
6. *Il arrivera lundi prochain.*
7. *C'est aujourd'hui lundi.*
8. *Venez samedi prochain.*
9. *l'hiver*
10. *dimanche*
11. *Nous sommes le vingt.*
12. *Samedi est le combien?*

13. *Je viendrai le quatorze juillet.*
14. *C'est aujourd'hui le premier juin.*
15. *La lettre est datée du six juin.*

1. Sunday
2. in a quarter of an hour
3. See you one of these days.
4. all day (long)
5. What's today?
6. in the summer
7. winter
8. What's the date Saturday?
9. Today's the twentieth.
10. Today's Monday.
11. Come next Saturday.
12. He'll arrive next Monday. He's arriving next Monday.
13. The letter is dated June 6th.
14. I'll come (on) the 14th of July.
15. Today is the first of June.

ANSWERS

1—5; 2—3; 3—4; 4—6; 5—2; 6—12; 7—10; 8—11; 9—7; 10—1; 11—9; 12—8; 13—14; 14—15; 15—13.

WORD STUDY

l'ambition (f.)	ambition
l'argument (m.)	argument
brillant	brilliant
la capitale	capital
le contact	contact
le département	department
la maman	mama
le monument	monument
l'obstacle (m.)	obstacle
récent	recent

DEVANT LE KIOSQUE DE JOURNAUX (AT THE NEWSSTAND)

—*Madame, donnez-moi le Figaro, s'il vous plaît. Mais je n'ai pas de monnaie. Pouvez-vous me rendre sur 100 francs?*[1]
"Madam, give me *Figaro,* please. However, I don't have any small change. Can you give me change for a hundred francs?"

—*Vous me donnerez cent sous demain, dit la marchande.*
"Give me a hundred sous tomorrow," the woman said.

—*Et si je suis écrasé ce soir?*
"But suppose I get run over tonight?"

—*Bah! Ça ne serait pas une bien grande perte!*
"So what! It wouldn't be a very great loss!"

[1] Notice how French punctuation in dialogues differs from English: (1) there are no quotation marks and (2) each change of speaker is indicated by a dash.

NOTES

Monnaie coins; change ("Money" is *argent*: *Je n'ai pas d'argent*. I haven't any money).

Mais but; however.

Rendre sur 100 francs ("to give back the change from") to change a hundred francs.

Un sou five centimes; *cent sous* five francs.

Marchand storekeeper; *marchande* (woman) storekeeper.

Ecraser to crush, run over; *si je suis écrasé* if I get run over.

LESSON 28

53. TO GO

(To Go)

ALLER	(TO GO)
je vais	I go
tu vas	you go
il va	he goes
elle va	she goes
on va	one goes
nous allons	we go
vous allez	you go
ils vont	they go (masc.)
elles vont	they go (fem.)

1. Some Common Expressions with *aller:*

Va
Go! *(fam.)*

Allez!
Go!

Allez lentement.
Go slowly.

Allez là-bas.
Go there.

N'y allez pas.
Don't go there.

N'allez pas là-bas.
Don't go over there.

Allez-y!
Go on ahead! Keep going!
Go on! Continue!

Allez le chercher.
Go look for it! Go get it!

Où allez-vous?
Where are you going?

Il faut y aller.
We have to go there. ("It's necessary to go there.")

Je vais à la gare.
I'm going to the station.

Je vais à la banque.
I'm going to the bank.

Je vais au théâtre.
I'm going to the theater.

Il va à la campagne.
He's going to the country.

Je vais chez Jean.
I'm going to John's place (home).

Je vais le faire.
I'm going to do it. I'll do it.

Je vais le voir.
I'm going to see it (him). I'll see it (him).

Je vais le lui dire.
I'm going to tell him. I'll tell him.

Il va venir.
He's going to come.

Comment allez-vous?
How are you? ("How do you go?")

Je vais bien, merci.
Well, thanks. Fine, thanks.

{**Ça va?**
{**Comment ça va?**
How are you? How are things?

Ça va.
Fine. All right. O.K.

2. Where Am I Going?

Où vais-je?
Where am I going?

Où vas-tu?
Where are you *(fam.)* going?

Où va-t-il?
Where is he going?

Où va-t-elle?
Where is she going?

Où allons-nous?
Where are we going?

Où allez-vous?
Where are you going?

Où vont-ils?
Where are they *(masc.)* going?

Où vont-elles?
Where are they *(fem.)* going?

54. A FEW SHORT PHRASES

Attention!
Watch out! Pay attention!

Prenez garde!
Be careful! Watch out! ("Take care!")

Vite.
Fast.

Plus vite.
Faster.

Pas si vite.
Not so fast.

Pas trop vite.
Not too fast.

Moins vite.
Slower ("less fast").

Plus lentement.
Slower.

Plus tôt.
Sooner.

Plus tard.
Later.

A plus tard.
See you later.

Dépêchez-vous.
Hurry up.

Ne vous dépêchez pas.
Don't hurry.

Je suis pressé.
I'm in a hurry.

Je ne suis pas pressé.
I'm not in a hurry.

Prenez votre temps.
Take your time.

Un instant!
Just a minute!

Dans un instant.
In a minute.

Tout à l'heure.
Right away. In a minute.

Bientôt.
Soon.

Je viens.
I'm coming.

Je viens tout de suite.
I'm coming right away.

LESSON 29

55. ONE, THEY, PEOPLE

(Useful Word Groups III)

On.
One. They. People.

On dit que . . .
They say that . . . It's said that . . . People say that . . .

On m'a dit que . . .
I've been told that . . .

On le dit.
They say it.

On dit que c'est vrai.
They say it's true.

On m'a dit.
I've been told.

On ne sait pas.
Nobody knows.

On parle français.
French spoken.

Ici on parle anglais.
English spoken here.

Parle-t-on l'anglais ici?
Do they speak English here?

Comment dit-on cela en français?
How do you say that in French?

Comment dit-on "Good Morning" en français?
How do you say "Good morning" in French?

Comment écrit-on ce mot en français?
How is this word written (spelled) in French?

On sonne à la porte.
Someone's ringing ("at the door").

On ferme.
They're closing.

Que joue-t-on ce soir au théâtre?
What's playing at the theater tonight?

Notice that *on* can often be translated by the English passive:

On dit que . . .
It's said that . . .

On m'a dit que . . .
I've been told that . . .

Comment écrit-on ce mot?
How is this word written?

QUIZ 18

1. *Je suis pressé.*
2. *Je viens tout de suite.*
3. *Tout à l'heure.*
4. *Dans un instant.*
5. *Prenez votre temps.*
6. *On sonne à la porte.*
7. *On m'a dit.*
8. *On ne sait pas.*
9. *Ici on parle anglais.*
10. *Comment dit-on cela en français?*

1. Right away.
2. In a minute.
3. I'm in a hurry.
4. I'm coming right away.
5. Someone's ringing.
6. Take your time.
7. Nobody knows.
8. I've been told.
9. How do you say that in French?
10. English spoken here.

ANSWERS

1—3; 2—4; 3—1; 4—2; 5—6; 6—5; 7—8; 8—7; 9—10; 10—9.

WORD STUDY

la balle	ball
le chèque	check
civil	civil
le corridor	corridor
l'éducation (f.)	education
l'effort (m.)	effort
logique	logical
l'omission (f.)	omission
la page	page
la table	table

56. A LITTLE AND A LOT

Peu.
A little.

Beaucoup ou peu.
A lot or a little.

Un peu.
A little.

Très peu.
Very little.

Un petit peu.
A very little.

Peu à peu.
Little by little.

C'est trop peu.
It's not enough.

Encore un peu.
A little bit more.

Il parle peu.
He doesn't talk much.

En voulez-vous peu ou beaucoup?
Do you want a little or a lot of it?

Restons-ici un peu.
Let's stay here a little.

Donnez-m'en un peu.
Give me a little of it.

Donnez-moi un peu d'eau.
Give me a little water.

Un tout petit peu.
A very little bit.

Je parle très peu le français.
I speak very little French.

Beaucoup.
Much. A lot.

Je n'ai pas beaucoup d'argent.
I haven't much money.

Je n'ai pas beaucoup de temps.
I haven't much time.

Je l'aime beaucoup.
I like him (her, it) a lot.

57. TOO MUCH

Trop.
Too. Too much.

C'est trop.
It's too much.

Pas trop.
Not too much.

Trop peu.
Too little.

Trop chaud.
Too hot.

Trop froid.
Too cold.

Trop d'eau.
Too much water.

58. MORE OR LESS

Plus ou moins.
More or less.

Au plus.
At the most.

Au moins.
At the least.

De plus en plus.
More and more.

De moins en moins.
Less and less.

Six fois plus.
Six times more.

Plus tôt.
Earlier.

Plus tard.
Later.

Plus chaud.
Hotter.

Plus cher.
More expensive.

Il n'y en a plus.
There's no more of it. There's no more of it left.

C'est plus que ça.
It's more than that.

C'est le livre le plus intéressant que je connaisse.
This is the most interesting book I know.

Il est plus grand que son frère.
He's taller than his brother.

Elle est plus grande que moi.
She's taller than I.

Elle n'est pas plus grande que moi.
She's not taller than I am.

Elle est moins grande que moi.
She's less tall than I (am).

Elle n'est pas aussi grande que moi.
She isn't as tall as I (am).

59. ENOUGH AND SOME MORE

Assez.
Enough.

Est-ce assez?
Is it enough?

C'est assez.
It's enough.

C'est plus qu'assez.
It's more than enough.

Ce n'est pas assez.
It's not enough.

C'est assez grand.
It's large enough. It's rather large.

Assez bien.
Fairly well. Rather well.

Avez-vous assez d'argent?
Do you have enough money?

Encore.
Some more.

Encore?
Some more?

Encore un peu.
A little more. Another little bit.

Encore un verre d'eau.
Another glass of water.

Encore du pain.
Some more bread.

Encore de la viande.
Some more meat.

Encore beaucoup.
Much more. Lots more.

Venez encore.
Come again.

Dites-le encore.
Say it again.

Répétez encore une fois, s'il vous plaît.
Please repeat it.

60. GOOD

C'est bon.
It's good.

C'est très bon.
It's very good.

Ce n'est pas bon.
It's not good.

Ce vin est bon.
This wine is good.

Cette viande est bonne.
This meat is good.

Ils sont bons.
They're good.

Elles sont bonnes.
They're *(fem.)* good.

Bonjour.
Hello! Good morning. Good afternoon. Good day.

Bon nuit.
Good night.

61. GOOD, WELL

Bien.
Good, well.

C'est très bien.
It's very good.

Ce n'est pas bien.
It's not very good.

Pas trop bien.
Not too good.

Très bien, monsieur.
Very well, sir.

Est-ce bien?
Is it good?

C'est bien fait.
It's well done (well made).

Je l'aime bien.
I like him (her, it) very much.

Je suis bien sûr.
I'm very sure.

Je suis bien content.
I'm very glad.

Tout va bien.
Everything's going well. Everything's all right.

Bien mieux.
Much better.

Bien plus.
Much more.

Bien moins.
Much less.

Bien cher.
Very (rather) expensive.

Bien tard.
Very (rather) late.

Bien tôt.
Very (rather) early.

Bien d'autres.
Many others.

Tout est bien qui finit bien.
All's well that ends well.

Eh bien?
Well? So what?

QUIZ 19

1. *Tout va bien.*
2. *C'est très bien.*
3. *Je suis bien sûr.*
4. *Je suis bien content.*
5. *En avez-vous assez?*
6. *Dites-le encore.*
7. *Répétez encore une fois s'il vous plaît.*
8. *Venez encore.*
9. *Je l'aime beaucoup.*
10. *Donnez-m'en un peu.*

1. It's very good.
2. Do you have enough of it?
3. Say it again.
4. Give me a little of it.
5. I like it a lot.
6. I'm very glad.
7. Everything's going well. Everything's all right.
8. I'm very sure.
9. Please repeat it.
10. Come again.

ANSWERS

1—7; 2—1; 3—8; 4—6; 5—2; 6—3; 7—9; 8—10; 9—5; 10—4.

WORD STUDY

anxieux	anxious
le chef	chief
la difficultè	difficulty
le docteur	doctor
l'épisode (m.)	episode
futur	future
glorieux	glorious
nerveux	nervous
la période	period
le peuple	people

62. BEAUTIFUL

Beau.
Beautiful.

C'est très beau.
It's very beautiful (nice, fine).

Pas très beau.
Not very beautiful.

Beau temps.
Nice weather.

Un beau pays.
A beautiful country.

Une belle journée.
A nice day.

Il fait beau.
It's nice out. The weather's nice.

Il est beau.
He's handsome.

Elle est belle.
She's beautiful (pretty).

Un bel homme.
A handsome man.

De belles femmes.
Beautiful women.

Ils ne sont pas beaux.
They're not handsome.

Beaux arts.
Fine arts.

Bel et bien.
Well and good.

Un bel ouvrage.
A beautiful job (piece of work).

Notice that the form *bel* is used before masculine singular nouns beginning with a vowel or *h* and that the masculine plural form is *beaux*.

63. LIKE, AS

Comme.
Like. As.

Comme moi.
Like me.

Comme ça.
Like this (that).

Comme les autres.
Like the others.

Comme ci, comme ça.
So, so.

Pas comme ça.
Not like this (that).

Comme ceci.
Like this.

C'est comme cela.
That's how it is. That's the way it is.

Comme vous voudrez.
As you wish.

Comme il est tôt!
How early (it is)!

Comme il est tard!
How late (it is)!

Comme c'est cher!
How expensive (it is)!

64. ALL

Tout.
All. Every.

Tout homme.
Every man.

Toute femme.
Every woman.

Tous les hommes.
All (the) men.

Toutes les femmes.
All (the) women.

Tout est ici.
Everything's here.

Toute la journée.
All day. The whole day.

Tous les jours.
Every day.

Tout est prêt.
Everything's ready.

Tous sont prêts.
All (masc.) are ready.

Toutes sont prêtes.
All (fem.) are ready.

Prenez-les tous.
Take all of them.

Nous sommes tous là.
We're all here.

C'est tout.
That's all. That's the whole lot. That'll do.

Est-ce tout?
Is that all? Is that everything? Is that the whole lot?

Tout le monde.
Everybody.

Tout de suite.
Right away. Just now.

Tout à l'heure.
A moment ago. In a moment.

A tout à l'heure.
See you soon. See you in a little while.

Tout à fait.
Completely.

Tout à fait mal.
Completely bad.

65. SOME, ANY, OF IT

En.
Some. Any. Of it.

En avez-vous?
Do you have any?

A-t-il de l'argent?
Does he have any money?

Oui, il en a.
Yes, he has (some).

Avez-vous d l'argent?
Do you have any money?

Non, je n'en ai pas.
No, I don't have any.

Nous n'en avons plus.
We don't have any more of it.

Voici de l'argent. Donnez-en à Jean.
Here's some money. Give some of it to John.

J'en ai assez.
I have enough of it (of them).

Donnez-m'en.
Give me some.

Donnez-nous en.
Give us some.

Donnez-lui en.
Give him some.

Donnez-leur en.
Give them some.

Je lui en ai donné.
I gave him some.

Je lui en ai parlé.
I spoke to her about it.

Avez-vous besoin de mon livre?
Do you need my book?

Oui, j'en ai besoin.
Yes, I need it.

Vient-il de Paris?
Is he coming from Paris?

Il en vient directement.
He's coming directly from there.

Il y en a.
There is (are) some.

Y en a-t-il encore?
Is (are) there any more?

Combien de livres avez-vous?
How many books do you have?

J'en ai dix.
I have ten (of them).

Ont-ils des livres?
Do they have any books?

Oui, ils en ont beaucoup.
Yes, they have lots (of them).

Non, ils n'en ont pas.
No, they haven't any.

Avez-vous de la viande?
Do you have any meat?

Oui, j'en ai.
I have some.

Qu'en pensez-vous?
What do you think of (about) it?

QUIZ 20

1. *Y en a-t-il encore?*
2. *Il y en a.*
3. *Avez-vous de l'argent?*
4. *En avez-vous?*
5. *Donnez-lui en.*
6. *Donnez m'en.*
7. *Non, ils n'en ont pas.*

8. *Qu'en pensez-vous?*
9. *Cette viande est bonne.*
10. *C'est bon.*
11. *Un bel ouvrage.*
12. *Beau temps.*
13. *C'est très beau.*
14. *Il fait beau.*
15. *Une belle journée.*

1. It's very beautiful (nice, fine).
2. Nice weather.
3. A nice day.
4. It's nice out. The weather's nice.
5. A beautiful job (work).
6. This meat is good.
7. It's good.
8. Do you have any?
9. Do you have any money?
10. Give me some.
11. Give him some.
12. There is (are) some.
13. Is (are) there any more?
14. No, they haven't any.
15. What do you think of it?

ANSWERS

1—13; 2—12; 3—9; 4—8; 5—11; 6—10; 7—14; 8—15; 9—6; 10—7; 11—5; 12—2; 13—1; 14—4; 15—3.

LESSON 30

66. SMALL TALK

(Small Talk)

Bien sûr.
Of course. Certainly.

Entendu!
Of course! Agreed! ("Understood!")

C'est entendu.
That's understood. That's settled. Agreed.

Bien entendu.
Of course. Naturally. Certainly.

En effet.
Indeed. In fact. In reality
As a reply to a statement:
That's so. That's true.

Tant pis.
So much the worse.

Tant mieux.
So much the better.

Je le crois.
I think so.

Je crois que non.
I don't think so.

D'accord!
Agreed!

Je suis d'accord.
I agree.

Je le suppose.
I suppose so.

Je suppose que non.
I suppose not.

Je l'espère.
I hope so.

J'espère que non.
I hope not.

Peut-être.
Perhaps.

Naturellement.
Naturally.

Certainement.
Certainly.

Certainement pas.
Certainly not.

C'est dommage!
It's a pity! It's a shame! Too bad!

Quel dommage!
What a pity! What a shame!

Ça dépend.
That depends.

Ça ne fait rien.
That's nothing. That's not important. That doesn't matter.

Ça ne fait rien du tout.
That doesn't matter at all.

Ça ne me fait rien.
It doesn't matter to me. I don't care.

Si ça ne vous fait rien.
If you have no objections. If it doesn't inconvenience you.

Ça m'est égal.
I don't care. It's all the same to me.

QUIZ 21

1. *C'est dommage.*
2. *Ça ne fait rien.*
3. *Ça ne me fait rien.*
4. *Ça dépend.*
5. *D'accord.*
6. *Entendu!*
7. *Je l'espère.*
8. *Bien sûr.*
9. *Je suis d'accord.*
10. *Je le suppose.*

1. Of course, certainly.
2. Of course! Agreed!
3. Agreed.
4. I agree.
5. I suppose so.
6. I hope so.
7. It's a pity (shame). Too bad!
8. That depends.
9. That's nothing. That's not important. That doesn't matter.
10. I don't care. It doesn't matter to me.

ANSWERS

1—7; 2—9; 3—10; 4—8; 5—3; 6—2; 7—6; 8—1; 9—4; 10—5.

67. THE SAME

Même.
The same.

C'est la même chose.
It's all the same thing.

Ce ne sont pas les mêmes.
These aren't the same.

En même temps.
At the same time.

Au même moment.
At the same moment.

Dans la même ville.
In the same town.

Enchanté!—Moi de même.
Glad to know you. The same here.

Je le fais moi-même.
I'm doing it myself.

Tu le fais toi-même.
You're *(fam.)* doing it yourself.

Il le fait lui-même.
He's doing it himself.

Elle le fait elle-même.
She's doing it herself.

Nous le faisons nous-mêmes.
We're doing it ourselves.

Vous le faites vous-mêmes.
You're doing it yourselves.

Ils le font eux-mêmes.
They're *(masc.)* doing it themselves.

Elles le font elles-mêmes.
They're *(fem.)* doing it themselves.

68. ALREADY

Déjà.
Already.

Il est déjà là.
He's already there.

Il est déjà fait ça.
He's already done that.

Est-il déjà parti?
Has he left already?

Avez-vous déjà fini?
Have you finished already?

WORD STUDY

l'attaque (f.)	attack
l'avantage (m.)	advantage
confortable	comfortable
le courage	courage
courageux	courageous
l'indépendance (f.)	independence
le langage	language
le message	message
l'opinion (f.)	opinion
le silence	silence

LESSON 31

69. LIKING AND DISLIKING

(Liking and Disliking)

1. I Like It.

Bon!
Good!

C'est bon.
It's good.

C'est très bon.
It's very good.

C'est beau.
It's beautiful.

C'est excellent.
It's excellent.

C'est magnifique.
It's excellent. It's wonderful.

C'est admirable.
It's admirable. It's wonderful.

C'est charmant.
It's very nice. It's charming. It's lovely.

C'est superbe.
It's wonderful.

C'est parfait.
It's perfect.

C'est formidable.
It's really something! Well, I never!

Ça me plaît.
I like that.

J'aime ça.
I like that.

Je l'aime bien.
I like it a lot.

Ça me plaît énormement.
I'm very pleased with it. I like it very much.

Il est très gentil.
He's very nice.

Elle est très gentille.
She's very nice.

Il est très aimable.
He is very pleasant (likable).

Elle est très aimable.
She is very pleasant (likable).

Vous êtes très aimable.
You're very kind. That's very kind of you.

2. I Don't Like It

Ce n'est pas bon.
It's not good *(of food, etc.)*.

Ce n'est pas bien.
It's not good. It's not nice.

C'est mauvais.
C'est mal.
It's bad.

Ce n'est pas beau.
It's not beautiful.

Ça ne vaut rien.
It's worthless.

Je ne l'aime pas.
I don't like it.

Je n'aime pas ça.
I don't like that.

Il ne me plaît pas.
I don't like him.

Ça ne me plaît pas.
I don't like that ("That doesn't please me.")
(Recording continued on page 160)

QUIZ 22

1. *Je n'aime pas ça.*
2. *C'est parfait.*
3. *C'est beau.*
4. *C'est formidable.*
5. *Ça me plaît énormement.*
6. *Il est très gentil.*
7. *J'ai perdu non chemin.*
8. *C'est mauvais.*
9. *Vous êtes très aimable.*
10. *C'est magnifique.*

1. It's excellent. It's wonderful.
2. It's really something! Well, I never!
3. I'm very pleased with it.
4. He's very nice.
5. You're very kind.
6. It's bad.
7. I've lost my way.
8. It's beautiful.
9. I don't like that.
10. It's perfect.

ANSWERS

1—9; 2—10; 3—8; 4—2; 5—3; 6—4; 7—7; 8—6; 9—5; 10—1.

REVIEW QUIZ 3

1. *Il l'a mis*—(in) *sa poche.*

   a. sur
   b. dans
   c. sous

2. *C'est*—(under) *la chaise.*

   a. dedans
   b. sous
   c. si

3. *Vous pouvez le faire*—(without) *aucune difficulté.*

   a. sans
   b. par
   c. si

4. *Je l'ai trouvé*—(under) *un tas de papiers.*

   a. sur
   b. sous
   c. dessus

5. *On dit que c'est*—(true).

   a. parle
   b. vrai
   c. cela

6. *Je*—(am going) *à la banque.*

   a. allez
   b. va
   c. vais

7. *Il*—(is going) *à la campagne.*

   a. va
   b. faut
   c. allez

8. *Donnez-moi un*—(little) *d'eau.*

   a. peu
   b. beaucoup
   c. ici

9. *Je n'ai pas*—(much) *d'argent.*

   a. peu
   b. beaucoup
   c. trop

10. *C'est*—(more) *que ça.*

    a. moins
    b. plus
    c. tôt

11. *Ce n'est pas*—(enough).

    a. encore
    b. bon
    c. assez

12. *Elle est*—(beautiful).

    a. bien
    b. belle
    c. bon

13. —(as) *vous voulez.*

    a. pas
    b. comme
    c. tôt

14. *Nous sommes*—(all) *là.*

    a. comme
    b. assez
    c. tous

15. —(everybody) *le sait.*

a. tout le monde
b. tout à l'heure
c. tout à fait

16. *Je*—(think) *que non.*

a. tenez
b. crois
c. suis

17. *J'*—(hope) *que non.*

a. mieux
b. espère
c. suppose

18. *Ça ne fait*—(nothing).

a. même
b. rien
c. déjà

19. *C'est la*—(same) *chose.*

a. même
b. déjà
c. naturellement

20. *Avez-vous*—(already) *fini?*

a. même
b. rien
c. déjà

ANSWERS

1—b; 2—b; 3—a; 4—b; 5—b; 6—c; 7—a; 8—a; 9—b; 10—b; 11—c; 12—b; 13—b; 14—c; 15—a; 16—b; 17—b; 18—b; 19—a; 20—c.

UN MOT POUR RIRE

Olive et Marius vont au restaurant et chacun commande un bifteck. Quelques instants plus tard le garçon revient avec un grand et un petit morceau de viande. Olive se précipite sur le grand morceau. Marius, furieux, lui dit:

Mal élevé, tu ne sais pas que tu aurais dû prendre le plus petit morceau puisque tu t'es servi d'abord?

Olive lui répond:

—Si tu avais été à ma place, quel morceau aurais-tu pris?

—Le plus petit, répond Marius, bien entendu!

—Alors, s'exclame Olive, de quoi te plains-tu puis-que tu l'as eu.

A WITTICISM

Olive and Marius go to a restaurant and each orders a steak. A few minutes later the waiter comes back with a large piece of meat and a small one. Olive seizes the large piece. Marius is furious and says to him:

"What bad manners you have! Don't you know that since you were the first to help yourself you should have taken the smaller piece?"

Olive answers:

"If you were in my place, which piece would you have taken?"

"The smaller one, of course," says Marius.

"Well then," Olive answers, "what are you complaining about? You have it, haven't you?"

NOTES

Un mot pour rire. "A word to laugh."

Revient comes back; from *revenir* to come back.

Mal élevé ill-bred; ill-bred person.

Tu aurais dû you should have; *tu aurais dû prendre* you should have taken.

Aurais-tu pris would you have taken.
Bien entendu of course.
Commande orders.
Se précipite hurries, hastens; seizes, grabs.
Te plains-tu do you complain *(fam.)*.
Puisque since.

70. WHO? WHAT? WHEN?

{*Que . . . ?*
{*Qu'est-ce que . . . ?*
What? . . .

Quel livre?
What book? Which book?

Quelle lettre?
What letter? Which letter?

Lequel?
Which one?

Quand?
When?

Qui?
Who?

Qui est-ce qui . . . ?
Who . . . ?

Quoi?
What?

Pourquoi?
Why?

Où?
Where?

Combien?
How much?

Comment?
How?

1. *Que* "What?"

{*Que . . . ?*
{*Qu'est-ce que . . . ?*
What? . . . ?

{*Que dites-vous?*
{*Qu'est-ce vous dites?*
What are you saying?

Qu'est-ce que vous dites de cela?
What do you say about that?

{*Qu'en dites vous?*
{*Qu'est-ce que vous en dites?*
What do you say about it?

{*Que faites-vous?*
{*Qu'est-ce que vous faites?*
What are you doing

{*Que voulez-vous?*
{*Qu'est-ce que vous voulez?*
What do you want? What would you like?

Qu'est-ce que vous voulez faire maintenant?
What do you want to do now?

{*Que voulez-vous dire?*
{*Qu'est-ce que vous voulez dire?*
What do you mean?

Qu'est-ce que vous cherchez?
What are you looking for?

{*Qu'avez-vous?*
{*Qu'est-ce que vous avez?*
What do you have? What's the matter with you? What's wrong with you?

{*Qu'a-t-il?*
{*Qu'est-ce qu'il a?*
What does he have? What's the matter with him?

Qu'est-ce que c'est?
What is it?

Qu'est-ce que c'est que ceci?
What's this?

Qu'est-ce que c'est que ça?
What's that?

Qu'est-ce qu'il y a?
What's the matter?

Qu'est-ce qui arrive?
What's going on? What's happening?

Qu'est-ce qui est arrivé?
What happened?

Qu'est-ce qui se passe?
What's happening? What's up?

Qu'importe?
What difference does it make? What does it matter?

Quel?
What *(masc.)*!

Quel homme?
What man?

Quels hommes?
What men?

Quel est votre nom?
What's your name?

Quel est votre nom?
What's your name?

Quel est le nom de cette ville?
What's the name of this town?

Quel est le nom de cette rue?
What's the name of this street?

Donnez-moi le livre.
Give me the book.

Quel livre?
What book? Which book?

Quel jour sommes-nous?
What's today? ("What day are we?")

Quel mois sommes-nous?
What month is it?

Quelle?
What *(fem.)*?

Quelle femme?
What woman?

Quelles femmes?
What women?

Quelle heure est-il?
What's the time? ("What's the hour?")

A quelle heure?
At what time? ("At what hour?")

Quelles nouvelles?
What's new?

Quelle différence!
What a difference!

Quelle est la différence entre les deux choses?
What's the difference between the two things?

2. *Lequel* "Which One?"

Lequel?
Which one?

Lequel est-ce?
Which one is it?

Lequel est-il?
Which is he (it)?

Lequel est le mien?
Which (one) is mine?

Lequel est meilleur?
Which (onc) is better?

Lequel est le meilleur?
Which (one) is the better one? Which (one) is best?

Lequel voulez-vous?
Which (one) do you want?

Lequel désirez-vous?
Which (one) do you want? Which (one) would you like?

Lequel a raison?
Which one (who) is right?

3. *Quand* "When?"

Quand?
When?

{*C'est quand?*
{*Quand est-ce?*
When is it?

A quand?
Until when?

Quand venez-vous?
When are you coming?

Quand partez-vous?
When are you leaving?

Quand va-t-il venir?
When is he going to come? When will he come?

Depuis quand êtes-vous ici?
How long have you been here?

4. *Qui* "Who?" "Whom?"

Qui?
Who?

Qui est-ce?
Who is it?

Qui êtes-vous?
Who are you?

{*Qui sait ça?*
{*Qui est-ce qui sait ça?*
Who knows that?

{*Qui vient avec nous?*
{*Qu'est-ce qui vient avec nous?*
Who's coming with us?

A qui est-ce?
Whose is it? ("To whom is it?")

Pour qui est-ce?
Who's it for?

A qui parlez-vous?
Who are you talking to?

De qui parlez-vous?
Who are you speaking about?

Avec qui venez-vous?
Who are you coming with?

Qui voulez-vous voir?
Who (Whom) do you want to see?

Qui est-ce que vous cherchez?
Who (Whom) are you looking for?

5. *Quoi* "What?"

Quoi?
What?

Avec quoi?
With what?

Sur quoi?
On what?

A quoi?
To what?

Quoi de neuf?
What's new?

A quoi pensez-vous?
What are you thinking about?

De quoi avez-vous besoin?
What do you need?

6. *Pourqoi* "Why?"

Pourquoi?
Why?

Et pourquoi pas?
And why not?

{*Pourquoi dites-vous ça?*
{*Pourquoi est-ce que vous dites ça?*
Why do you say that?

Pourquoi a-t-il[1] fait ça?
Why did he do it?

7. *Comment* "How?"

Comment?
How?

Mais comment?
But how?

Comment ça?
How's that? What do you mean?

[1] For the *t* see page 31.

Comment vous appelez-vous?
What's your name? ("How do you call yourself?")

Comment ça va?
How are you?

Comment dites-vous?
What did you say? ("What are you saying?")

Comment écrit-on ce mot en français?
How do you write this word in French? How's this word written in French?

Comment dit-on cela en anglais?
How do you say that in English?

Comment dites-vous "Thanks" en français?
How do you say "Thanks" in French?

Comment dit-on en français "Thanks?"
What's the French for "Thanks?" How do you say "Thanks" in French?

Comment est-ce arrivé?
How did it happen?

Comment y va-t-on?
How does one go about it?

C'est fait comment?
How's it made?

Comment l'avez-vous fait?
How did you do (make) it?

Comment y aller?
How do you go there ("How to go there?")

Comment faire?
What's to be done? What can one do? ("How to do?")

QUIZ 23

1. *Qu'est-ce que vous faites?*
2. *Qu'est-ce que vous voulez?*
3. *Qu'est-ce qu'il y a?*
4. *Que voulez-vous dire?*
5. *Qu'est-ce que vous cherchez?*
6. *Quel est le nom de cette rue?*
7. *Qu'importe?*
8. *Quelle différence!*
9. *Lequel est le meilleur?*
10. *Quand partez-vous?*
11. *Qui êtes-vous?*
12. *Qui voulez-vous voir?*
13. *De quoi avez-vous besoin?*
14. *Pourquoi a-t-il fait ça?*
15. *Mais comment?*
16. *Comment ça va?*
17. *Pourquoi dites-vous ça?*
18. *Et pourquoi pas?*
19. *Quoi de neuf?*
20. *Comment vous appelez-vous?*

1. What's new?
2. What do you need?
3. And why not?
4. Why do you say that?
5. Why did he do it?
6. What's your name?
7. How are you?
8. But how?
9. When are you leaving?
10. Who are you?
11. Whom do you want to see?
12. What a difference!
13. Which is the best?
14. What do you mean?
15. What are you looking for?
16. What's the matter?

17. What difference does it make? What does it matter?
18. What's the name of this street?
19. What are you doing?
20. What do you want?

ANSWERS

1—19; 2—20; 3—16; 4—14; 5—15; 6—18; 7—17; 8—12; 9—13; 10—9; 11—10; 12—11; 13—2; 14—5; 15—8; 16—7; 17—4; 18—3; 19—1; 20—6.

WORD STUDY

comique	comic
le coton	cotton
le détail	detail
l'employé (m.)	employee
le jugement	judgment
le muscle	muscle
le parc	park
le restaurant	restaurant
le rose	rose
la trace	trace

71. HOW MUCH?

Le prix?
The price?

{**Quel prix?**
{**C'est quel prix?**
What's the price?

Combien?
How much?

{**C'est combien?**
{**Combien est-ce?**
How much is it?

Combien pour le tout?
How much for everything? How much does it all cost?

C'est combien la pièce?
How much each?

C'est combien la douzaine?
How much a dozen?

Combien en voulez-vous?
How many do you want? How much do you want for it?

72. HOW MANY?

Combien?
How many?

Combien d'argent?
How much (money)?

Combien d'hommes?
How many men?

Combien de temps?
How much time? How long?

Combien de temps faut-il pour y aller?
How long ("how much time") does it take to get there?

Combien y en a-t-il?
How many are there ("of it, them")?

Combien y a-t-il d'ici à la gare?
How far is it from here to the station?

Combien en reste-t-il?
Il en reste combien?
How many are left ("of them")?

Combien en avez-vous?
Vous en avez combien?
How many of them do you have?

Nous sommes le combien?
Le combien sommes-nous?
What's the date today? ("We are the how many?")

Lundi ce sera le combien?
What's the date Monday? ("Monday will be the how many?")

QUIZ 24

1. *Combien y en a-t-il?*
2. *Combien est-ce?*
3. *Combien en voulez-vous?*
4. *Quel prix?*
5. *Combien de temps?*
6. *Le combien sommes-nous?*
7. *Combien en reste-t-il?*
8. *Combien en avez-vous?*
9. *C'est quel prix?*
10. *Lundi ça sera le combien?*

1. How many remain (of it, them)?
2. What's the date today? ("We are the how many?")
3. What's the date Monday?
4. What's the price?
5. What's the price?
6. How much is it?
7. How many do you want? How much do you want for it?
8. How much time? How long?
9. How many of them do you have?
10. How many are there (of it, them)?

ANSWERS

1—10; 2—6; 3—7; 4—5; 5—8; 6—2; 7—1; 8—9; 9—4; 10—3.

LESSON 32

73. Useful Word Groups

(Useful Word Groups IV)

1. Some, Someone, Something.

Quelque.
Some.

Quelque argent.
Some money.

Quelque chose.
Something.

Quelque chose de nouveau.
Something new.

Quelques hommes.
Some men.

Quelques mots.
Some words. A few words.

Quelqu'un.
Someone.

Y a-t-il quelqu'un qui peut le faire?
Is there anyone who can do it?

Quelquefois.
Sometimes.

Je le vous quelquefois.
I see him sometimes.

2. Once, Twice

Fois.
A time.

Une fois.
Once. One time.

Deux fois.
Twice. Two times.

La première fois.
The first time.

La prochaine fois.
The next time.

La dernière fois.
The last time.

Encore une fois.
Another time. Again. Once more.

Toutes les fois.
Every time. Each time.

Cette fois-ci.
This time.

3. Up to

Jusque.
Up to.

Jusqu'ici.
Up to now.

Jusque là.
Up to there.

Jusqu'au bout.
To the end.

Jusqu'à la gare.
Up to (as far as) the station.

Jusqu'à ce soir.
Up to this evening.

Jusqu'à demain.
Up to tomorrow.

Jusqu'à lundi.
Up to Monday.

4. I Need It

J'ai besoin de cela.
I need it (that).

Il n'a pas besoin de celui-ci.
He doesn't need this one.

Avez-vous besoin de quelque chose?
Do you need anything?

Je n'ai besoin de rien.
I don't need anything.

Je n'en ai pas du tout besoin.
I don't need it at all.

5. It's Necessary

Il faut absolument que je vous vois.
It's absolutely necessary that I see you.

Il faut le lui dire.
You have to tell him.

Il faut rentrer de bonne heure.
You must come home early.

Il faut admettre la vérité.
One must recognize the truth.

6. I Feel Like

J'en ai envie.
I'd like to have it. I feel like having it.

Je n'ai pas envie d'y aller.
I don't feel like going there.

J'ai envie de manger de la glace.
I feel like having some ice cream.

Avez-vous envie de voir ce film?
Would you like to see this (that) movie?

7. At the Home of

Chez.
At the home of.

Nous étions chez des amis.
We were at the home of some friends.

Je vous verrai chez les Durand.
I'll see you at the Durands'.

Venez chez nous.
Come over to our place.

Quand j'habitais chez mon père.
When I was living with my father.

Monsieur Durand est-il chez lui?
Is Mr. Durand at home?

Je dois aller chez le docteur.
I have to go to the doctor's.

Faites comme chez vous.
Make yourself at home.

8. Here It Is

Voici!
Here! Here it is!

Me voici.
Here I am.

Le voici.
Here he is.

La voici.
Here she is.

Les voice.
Here they are.

Voici le livre.
Here's the book.

9. There It Is!

Voilà!
There it is

Le voilà.
There he is.

La voilà.
There she is.

Les voilà.
There they are.

Vous voilà.
There you are.

Voilà la réponse.
That's the answer.

QUIZ 25

1. *Quelque argent.*	1. To the end.
2. *Une fois.*	2. I need that.
3. *Jusqu'au bout.*	3. Here's the book.
4. *J'ai besoin de cela.*	4. Some money.
5. *Voici le livre.*	5. Once.

ANSWERS

1—4; 2—5; 3—1; 4—2; 5—3.

WORD STUDY

bleu	blue
la copie	copy
le couple	couple
le cousin	cousin
le double	double
le parfum	perfume
la route	route
sûr	sure
la surface	surface
vigoureux	vigorous

REVIEW QUIZ 4

1. ——— (what) *est le nom de cette ville?*

a. lequel
b. quel
c. quand

2. ——— (who) *êtes vous?*

a. qui
b. quel
c. quoi

3. ——— (when) *va-t-il venir?*

a. qui
b. quand
c. quel

4. ——— (why) *est-ce que vous dites ça?*

a. quelque
b. quand
c. pourquoi

5. Le ——— (twelfth) *chapitre.*

a. douzième
b. dix-septième
c. sixième

6. Ce chapeau m'a coûte ——— (fifty-four) *francs.*

a. deux
b. cinquante
c. cinquante-quatre

7. J'habite au numéro ——— (seventeen) *de la rue Balzac.*

a. trente-trois
b. dix-sept
c. treize

8. *Il est* —— (noon).

   a. midi
   b. minuit
   c. onze heures

9. *Nous nous verrons à* —— (six) *heures.*

   a. cinq
   b. sept
   c. six

10. *Il est* —— (time) *de le faire.*

    a. combien
    b. temps
    c. ici

11. *Nous sommes aujourd'hui* —— (Wednesday).

    a. mardi
    b. mercredi
    c. lundi

12. *Il partira* —— (Tuesday) *prochain.*

    a. mardi
    b. jeudi
    c. dimanche

13. *C'est aujourd'hui le premier* —— (June).

    a. juin
    b. julliet
    c. août

14. *Il n'a pas* —— (need) *de celui-ci.*

    a. cela
    b. besoin
    c. tout

15. ——— (how) *écrit-on ce mot en français?*

a. pourquoi
b. comment
c. cela

16. *Je suis né le* ——— (twelve) *avril.*

a. mai
b. onze
c. douze

17. ——— (here's) *le livre.*

a. voici
b. voilà
c. nous

18. *J'ai perdu mon* ——— (way).

a. cabine
b. chemin
c. court

19. *Il travaille du* ——— (morning) *au soir.*
a. matin
b. nuit
c. jour

20. *A quelle station dois-je* ——— (get off)?

a. sommes
b. descendre
c. encore

ANSWERS

1—b; 2—a; 3—b; 4—c; 5—a; 6—c; 7—b; 8—a; 9—c; 10—b; 11—b; 12—a; 13—a; 14—b; 15—b; 16—c; 17—a; 18—b; 19—a; 20—b.

LESSON 33

74. GETTING AROUND

(Getting Around)

Pardon.
Pardon me.

Excusez-moi.
Excuse me.

Quel est le nom de cette ville?
What is the name of this town?

A combien de kilomètres de Paris sommes-nous?
How far are we from Paris?

Combien de kilomètres y a-t-il d'ici à Paris?
How many kilometers from here to Paris?

C'est à dix kilomètres d'ici.
It's ten kilometers from here.

C'est à vingt kilomètres d'ici.
It's twenty kilometers from here.

Comment puis-je aller d'ici à Paris?
How do I get to Paris from here?

Suivez cette route.
Follow this road.

Pouvez-vous m'indiquer comment je puis me rendre à cette adresse?
Can you tell me how I can get to this address?

Pouvez-vous me dire comment je puis aller à cet endroit?
Can you tell me how I can get to this place?

Quel est le nom de cette rue?
What is the name of this street?

Pouvez-vous m'indiquer où se trouve cette rue?
Can you tell me where this street is?

Où est la rue Boileau?
Where is Boileau Street?

Est-ce loin d'ici?
Is it far from here?

Est-ce près d'ici?
Is it near here?

C'est la troisième rue à droite.
It's the third block to the right.

Allez par ici.
Go this way.

Allez droit devant vous.
Go straight ahead.

Allez au coin et prenez la première à gauche.
Go to the corner and turn left. ("Take the first street to the left.")

Prenez la première à droite.
Turn right. ("Take the first street to the right.")

Où se trouve le garage?
Where is the garage?

Où se trouve le commissaire de police?
Where is the police station?

Où se trouve la mairie?
Where is City Hall?

Où se trouve l'arrêt de l'autobus?
Where is the bus stop?

A quel arrêt dois-je descendre?
What station do I get off?

Où dois-je descendre?
Where do I get off?

Où se trouve la gare?
Where is the railroad station?

Où puis-je prendre le train pour Paris?
Where do I get the train for Paris?

Sur la voie numéro deux.
On track two.

Le train vient de partir.
The train just left.

LESSON 34

75. WRITING, PHONING, TELEGRAPHING

(Writing, Phoning, Telegraphing)

Quelle est l'heure de départ du prochain train?
At what time does the next train leave?

Un billet aller et retour pour Paris, s'il vous plaît.
May I have a round-trip ticket for Paris?

Combien est-ce?
How much is that?

Cinquante francs, vingt-cinq centimes.
Fifty francs, twenty-five centimes.

Combien de temps faut-il pour aller jusque là?
How long does it take to get there?

Un peu plus d'une heure.
A little over an hour.

Je voudrais écrire une lettre.
I'd like to write a letter.

Avez-vous un crayon?
Do you have a pencil?

Avez-vous un stylo?
Do you have a pen?

Avez-vous un buvard?
Do you have a blotter?

Avez-vous une enveloppe?
Do you have an envelope?

Avez-vous un timbre?
Do you have a stamp?

Où puis-je acheter un timbre?
Where can I buy a stamp?

Est-ce que vous avez un timbre par avion?
Do you have an air-mail stamp?

Où se trouve la poste?
Where is the post office?

Je voudrais envoyer cette lettre.
I'd like to mail this letter.

Combien de timbres faut-il mettre sur cette lettre?
How many stamps do I need on this letter?

Où se trouve la boîte aux lettres?
Where is a mailbox?

Où se trouve la boîte aux lettres le plus proche?
Where is the nearest mailbox?

Au coin de la rue.
On the corner.

Je voudrais envoyer un télégramme.
I'd like to send a telegram.

Où est-ce que je peux[1] envoyer un télégramme?
Where can I send a telegram?

[1] Notice that there are two ways of saying "I can": *je peux* and *je puis*. "Can I?" however is always *puis-je?*

Où se trouve le bureau de télégraphe?
Where is the telegraph office?

C'est au bureau de poste.
It's in the post office.

Combien coûte un télégramme pour Paris?
How much is a telegram to Paris?

Combien de temps cela prendra-t-il pour arriver?
How long will it take to get there?

Y a-t-il un téléphone ici?
Is there a phone here?

Où puis-je téléphoner?
Where can I phone?

Où se trouve le téléphone?
Where is the telephone?

Où a-t-il des cabines téléphoniques publiques?
Where are the phone booths?

Au bureau de tabac.
In the tobacco shop.

LESSON 35

(Family Affairs I)

Puis-je me servir de votre téléphone, s'il vous plaît?
May I use your phone?

Bien entendu!
Of course, go ahead!

Mlle,[1] puis-je avoir l'inter, s'il vous plaît?
May I have long distance, please?

Combien coûte la communication pour Paris?
How much is a telephone call to Paris?

[1] *Mlle* is the abbreviation for Mademoiselle.

Mlle, je voudrais Trudaine quarante-deux, cinquante-huit.
May I have Trudaine 4258.

Attendez un instant.
Hold the wire a minute.

Ce n'est pas libre.
The line's busy.

Mlle, vous m'avez donné un faux numéro.
Operator, you gave me the wrong number.

On ne répond pas.
There is no answer.

Puis-je parler à M.[1] Delacroix, s'il vous plaît?
May I speak to Mr. Delacroix, please?

C'est moi.
Speaking.

C'est M. Charpentier à l'appareil.
This is Mr. Charpentier speaking.

76. FAMILY AFFAIRS

Comment vous appelez-vous?
What is your name?

Je m'appelle Jean Granier.
My name is John Granier.

Comment s'appelle-t-il?
What is his name?

Il s'appelle Charles Lenoir.
His name is Charles Lenoir.

Comment s'appelle-t-elle?
What is her name?

[1] M. is the abbreviation for Monsieur.

Elle s'appelle Claire Durand.
Her name is Claire Durand.

Comment s'appellent-ils?
What are their names?

Il s'appelle Lucien Blamont, et elle s'appelle Marie Delacourt.
His name is Lucien Blamont and hers is Marie Delacourt.

Quel est son prénom?
What's his first name?

Son prénom est Jean.
His first name is John.

Quel est son nom de famille?
What's his last name?

Son nom de famille est Granier.
His last name is Granier.

D'où venez-vous?
Where are you from?

Je viens de Paris.
I'm from Paris.

Où êtes-vous né?
Where were you born?

Je suis né à Marseille.
I was born in Marseilles.

LESSON 36

(Family Affairs II)

Quel âge avez-vous?
How old are you?

J'ai vingt-quatre ans.
I'm twenty-four.

J'aurai vingt-quatre ans en septembre.
I'll be twenty-four in September.

Je suis né le dix-neuf août mil neuf cent seize.
I was born August 19, 1916.

Combien de frères avez-vous?
How many brothers do you have?

J'ai deux frères.
I have two brothers.

L'aîné a vingt-deux ans.
The older one is twenty-two.

Il va à l'université.
He's at the University.

Le plus jeune a dix-sept ans.
The younger one is seventeen.

Il est en première au lycée.
He's in the last year of the lycée.

Combien de soeurs avez-vous?
How many sisters do you have?

J'ai une soeur.
I have one sister.

Elle a quinze ans.
She's fifteen.

Elle est en troisième au lycée.
She's in the ninth grade of the lycée.

Qu'est-ce que fait votre père?
What does your father do?

Il est avocat.
He's a lawyer.

Il est architecte.
He's an architect.

Il est professeur.
He's a teacher.

Il est professeur d'université.
He's a university professor.

Il est docteur.
He's a doctor.

Il est dans les affaires.
He's in business.

Il est dans les textiles.
He's in the textile business.

Il est fermier.
He's a farmer.

Il est fonctionnaire.
He's a government employee.

C'est un ouvrier.
He's a worker.

Il travaille dans une usine d'automobiles.
He works in an automobile factory.

Quelle est la date de votre anniversaire?
When is your birthday?

Dans deux semaines, le vingt-trois janvier, ce sera mon anniversaire.
My birthday is in two weeks, January 23rd.

Est-ce que vous avez de la famille ici?
Do you have any relatives here?

Est-ce que toute votre famille habite ici?
Does all your family live here?

Toute ma famille sauf mes grandsparents.
All my family except my grandparents.

Ils habitent dans une ferme, près de Compiègne.
They live on a farm, near Compiegne.

Etes-vous parent avec M. Blamont?
Are you related to Mr. Blamont?

C'est mon oncle.
He's my uncle.

C'est mon cousin.
He's my cousin.

Etes-vous parent avec Mme[1] Delacourt?
Are you related to Madame Delacourt?

C'est ma tante.
She's my aunt.

C'est ma cousine.
She's my cousin.

[1]*Mme* is the abbreviation for Madame.

REVIEW QUIZ 5

1. *Quel est le nom de* —— (this) *ville?*

    a. cet
    b. ce
    c. cette

2. —— (how) *puis-je aller d'ici à Paris?*

    a. combien
    b. comment
    3. quel

3. —— (what) *est le nom de cette rue?*
    a. que
    b. qui
    c. quel

4. —— (where) *est la rue Boileau?*

    a. où
    b. quand
    c. que

5. —— (go) *par ici.*

    a. allez
    b. aller
    c. allons

6. *Allez au coin et prenez la première à* —— (left).

    a. gauche
    b. droite
    c. loin

7. —— (how much) *est-ce?*

    a. comment
    b. combien
    c. que

8. *Je voudrais* —— (to write) *une lettre.*

   a. écrivez
   b. écrire
   c. écrive

9. *Où puis-je acheter un* —— (stamp).

   a. timbre
   b. poste
   3. buvard

10. *Au coin de la* —— (street).

   a. rue
   b. ici
   c. avenue

11. —— (there) *a-t-il un téléphone ici?*

   a. y
   b. là
   c. ça

12. *Mlle, vous m'avez donné un* —— (wrong) *numéro.*

   a. faux
   b. faut
   c. pas

13. *Quel est son* —— (first name)?

   a. prénom
   b. famille
   c. appelle

14. *Où êtes-vous* —— (born)?
   a. ne
   b. né
   c. ni

15. *Le plus jeune a dix-sept* —— (years).

a. ans
b. an
c. année

16. *Il est* —— (lawyer).

a. professeur
b. avocat
c. fonctionnaire

17. *C'est un* —— (worker).

a. ouvrier
b. travaille
c. usine

18. *Ils habitent dans une ferme,* —— (near) *de Compiègne.*

a. pres
b. très
c. loin

19. —— (follow) *cette route.*

a. allez
b. suivez
c. prenez

20. *Est-ce* —— (far) *d'ici?*

a. loin
b. coin
c. près

21. *Sur la* —— (track) *numéro deux.*

a. voie
b. retour
c. train

22. *C'est* —— (I).

a. moi

b. je
c. mien

23. *Ce n'est pas* —— (free).

a. libre
b. livre
c. faux

24. *Etes-vous* —— (related) *avec M. Blamont?*

a. parent
b. sauf
c. famille

25. *Toute ma famille* —— (except) *mes grandsparents.*

a. sauf
b. sera
c. usine

ANSWER

1—c; 2—b; 3—c; 4—a; 5—a; 6—a; 7—b; 8—b; 9—a; 10—a; 11—a; 12—a; 13—a; 14—b; 15—a; 16—b; 17—a; 18—a; 19—b; 20—a; 21—a; 22—a; 23—a; 24—a; 25—a.

LESSON 37

EVERYDAY FRENCH CONVERSATION

(Shopping, Ordering a Meal)

77. SHOPPING

Emplettes
Purchases

1. **C'est combien?**
   How much is it?
2. **Dix francs.**
   Ten francs.
3. **C'est trop cher. Vous n'avez rien d'autre?**
   It's too expensive. Haven't you anything else?
4. **Dans le même genre?**
   Of the same kind?
5. **Oui, dans le même genre ou bien quelque chose d'approchant.**
   Yes, the same kind or something similar.
6. **Il y a ceci.**
   We have this.
7. **Vous n'avez rien d'autre à me montrer?**
   Don't you have anything else to show me?
8. **De moins cher?**
   Less expensive?
9. **Si possible.**
   If possible.
10. **Est-ce que ceci vous plairait?**
    Would you like this?

11. **Ça dépend du prix.**
That depends on the price.

12. **C'est huit francs.**
This is eight francs.

13. **Et ceci, c'est moins cher ou plus cher?**
How about this? Is it cheaper or more expensive?

14. **Plus cher.**
More expensive.

15. **Vous n'avez rien d'autre?**
Haven't you anything else?

16. **Pas pour l'instant, mais j'attends des nouveautés.**
Not at the moment, but I'm expecting some new styles soon.

17. **Quand ça?**
When?

18. **D'un jour à l'autre. Passez vers la fin de la semaine.**
Any day now. Drop in toward the end of the week.

19. **Certainement. Et ça c'est combien?**
I'll do that. By the way, how much is this?

20. **Deux francs la paire.**
Two francs a pair.

21. **Donnez-m'en une douzaine.**
Let me have a dozen.

22. **Voulez-vous les emporter?**
Will you take them with you?

23. **Non, faites-les moi livrer, s'il vous plaît.**
No, please have them delivered.

24. Toujours à la même adresse?
Still at the same address?

25. Oui, c'est toujours la même.
It's still the same.

26. Merci beaucoup. Au revoir, Madame.
Thank you very much. Good-by.

27. Au revoir.
Good-by.

NOTES

Title: *Emplettes*. Purchases.

1. *C'est combien?* "It's how much?"[1] — *C'est quel prix?* "It's what price?" — *Ça revient à combien?* "It comes to how much?"
2. *Dix* ten and *six* six are pronounced "dees" and "sees" when they stand by themselves. They are pronounced "dee" and "see" when they come before a noun beginning with a consonant, "deez" and "seez" when they come before a noun beginning with a vowel or *h*. (see page 34).
3. *Rien d'autre* nothing else. Notice the use of *de (d'* in this case because it comes before a vowel).
5. *Quelque chose d'approchant* ("something approaching") something like it. Notice that *quelque chose* is followed by *de* "of." *Approcher* to approach, come near.
6. *Il y a ceci.* "There is this."
10. *Plairait* would please you; from *plaire* to please.
12. *Huit* eight is pronounced "wee" before nouns beginning with a consonant and "weet" before nouns beginning with a vowel or *h* (see page 90).

[1] Words in quotation marks are literal translations.

13. "And this, is it less expensive or more expensive?"

15. *Rien d'autre*. Nothing else. Notice the use of *de (d')*.

16. *Attendre* to expect. *Nouveautés* novelties; new styles. *Nouveauté de la saison*. Latest style.

17. "When's that?"

18. "From one day to the other."—*Passer* to pass.—*La fin de la semaine* the end of the week. *La fin de la journée* the end of the day. *La fin du mois* the end of the month. *La fin de l'année* the end of the year.

23. *Faites!* Make! Do!; from *faire* to make, do (see page 214). *Faites-les moi livrer*. Have them delivered to me.

24. *Toujours* always. *Toujours* sometimes translates our "still": *Toujours à la même adresse?* Still the same address? *Est-il toujours à Paris?* Is he still in Paris?—Notice that *adresse* has only one *d* in French.

27. Common expressions for "good-by" are: *(formal) Au revoir, Adieu* (used when one doesn't ever expect to see a person again or not for a very long time), *Au plaisir* Till I see you again, *(more familiar) A la prochaine fois* "Until the next time," *A demain* "Until tomorrow," *A bientôt* See you soon. *A tout à l'heure* See you soon.

QUIZ 26

1. *C'est* —— (how much)?

    a. combien
    b. comment
    c. quand

2. *Dans le même* —— (kind).

    a. genre
    b. chose
    c. cher

3. *Oui, dans le même genre* —— (or) *bien quelque chose d'approchant.*

    a. quand
    b. ou
    c. que

4. *Il y a* —— (this).

    a. ce
    b. ça
    c. ceci

5. *De* —— (less) *cher.*

    a. mais
    b. moins
    c. rien

6. —— (that) *dépend du prix.*

    a. ça
    b. ceci
    c. ci

7. *Pas pour l'instant,* —— (but) *j'attends des nouveautés.*

    a. ou
    b. mais
    c. ça

8. ——— (when) *ça?*

a. comment
b. combien
c. quand

9. *Donnez-m'* ——— (of them) *une douzaine.*

a. y
b. en
c. ou

10. *Non, faites-* ——— (them) *moi livrer, s'il vous plaît.*

a. les
b. leurs
c. en

ANSWERS

1—a; 2—a; 3—b; 4—c; 5—b; 6—a; 7—b; 8—c; 9—b; 10—a.

78. ORDERING BREAKFAST

Le petit déjeuner
Breakfast

1. **G:[1] Tu dois avoir faim.**
   G: You must be hungry.

2. **Mme G: Oui, je prendrais bien quelque chose.**
   Mrs. G: Yes, I could certainly eat something.

3. **G: Il y a un bon restaurant à l'hôtel.**
   G: There's a good restaurant at the hotel.

4. **Mme G: C'est une bonne idée, allons-y.**
   Mrs. G: That's a good idea. Let's go there.

5. **G: Garçon! Garçon!**
   G: Waiter!

6. **W: Vous désirez, Madame, Monsieur?**
   W: Yes?

7. **G: Le petit déjeuner.**
   G: We'd like breakfast.

8. **Mme G: Qu'est-ce que vous donnez d'habitude?**
   Mrs. G: What do you have?

9. **W: Café au lait, ou thé au citron, ou au lait, ou bien du chocolat.**
   W: Coffee, tea with lemon or cream, or else hot chocolate.

10. **Mme G: Et avec cela?**
    Mrs. G: What else?

11. **W: Des petits pains ou croissants ou brioches.**
    W: Rolls or croissants or brioches.

[1] *G.* stands for *Monsieur Granier, Mme G.* for *Madame Granier. W.* stands for "Waiter."

12. **Mme G: Pas de beurre?**
Mrs. G: No butter?
13. **W: Si, Madame, du beurre et de la confiture.**
W: Of course, butter and jelly.
14. **Mme G: Je voudrais du café au lait et des croissants.**
Mrs. G: I'd like some coffee and some croissants.
15. **G: Donnez-moi la même chose et aussi un oeuf.**
G: Let me have the same and an egg as well.
16. **W: Très bien, monsieur. Monsieur désire-t-il quelque chose d'autre?**
W: Certainly, sir. Would you like anything else ?
17. **G: Non, c'est tout.**
G: No, that'll be all.
18. **Mme G: Garçon, une serviette, je vous prie.**
Mrs. G: Waiter, may I have a napkin, please?
19. **G: Voulez-vous aussi me donner une fourchette?**
G: Can you also let me have a fork?
20. **Mme G: Un peu plus de sucre aussi, s'il vous plaît.**
Mrs. G: And some more sugar, please.
21. **W: Voilà, Madame.**
W: Here you are, Madam.
22. **Mme G: Mon café est froid. Apportez-m'en un autre, s'il vous plaît.**
Mrs. G: My coffee is cold. Please bring me another cup.
23. **W: Avec plaisir.**
W: Gladly.
24. **G: Garçon, l'addition.**
G: Waiter, may I have the check?

25. **W: Voilà, monsieur.**
W: Here you are, sir.

26. **G: Voici. Gardez la monnaie.**
G: Here, keep the change.

27. **W: Merci beaucoup, monsieur. Au revoir, Madame.**
W: Thank you very much, sir. Good-by, Madam.

28. **G: Au revoir.**
G: Good-by.

NOTES

Title: *Le petit déjeuner.* Breakfast.

1. *Tu dois* you must, you ought to, you should; from *devoir* (see page 256). *Devoir* also means to owe. *Tu dois cent francs.* You owe me a hundred francs. For the use of *tu,* see page 29.

2. *Je prendrais* I would take; from *prendre* to take (see page 229). *Bien* well. *Bien* can often be translated "certainly."

5. *Garçon* waiter. The word also means *boy: Est-ce un garçon ou une fille?* Is it a boy or a girl? *Un petit garçon* a little boy. Also *fellow: C'est un bon garçon.* He's a nice fellow.

6. *Vous désirez?* "You desire?"

7. *Le petit déjeuner* breakfast. *Le déjeuner* lunch. *Le dîner* dinner.

8. "What do you usually serve ('give')?" means "What does your standard breakfast consist of?"

9. *Café au lait* ("coffee with milk") is served with the milk already in it. In small cafés you can also ask for a *café crème* but this too has milk rather than cream. Coffee and cream is served only in the better hotels and in some dairies.

10. "And with that?"

11. *Des petits pains.* Rolls. For the use of *des* see page 44.

13. *Si* yes. *Si* is used for *yes* when it contradicts the previous statement.

15. *Un oeuf* an egg. *Des oeufs* eggs. *Un oeuf à la coque* ("egg in a shell") a soft-boiled egg. *Un oeuf dur* a hard-boiled egg. *Un oeuf sur le plat* ("an egg on the plate") a fried egg. *Des oeufs brouillés* scrambled eggs. *Un oeuf poché* a poached egg.

18. *Je vous prie* "I beg you."

20. *Un peu plus de sucre* a little more sugar. Notice the use of *de*. *S'il vous plaît* ("if it pleases you") please. Abbreviated to *s.v.p.*: *Fermez la porte, s.v.p.* Please close the door. *Tournez le bouton, s.v.p.* Please turn the knob.

26. *La monnaie* small change. "Money" is *l'argent*.

79. A SAMPLE MENU

Menu

Potage aux légumes
Omelette aux fines herbes
Poulet rôti
Haricots verts
Pommes de terre Parisienne
Salade
Crêpes Suzette
Fromages variés
Café et liqueurs

Menu

Vegetable Soup
Omelet ("with savory herbs")
Roast Chicken
String Beans
Boiled Potatoes
Salad
Crêpes Suzette
Different Kinds of Cheese
Coffee and Liqueurs

REVIEW QUIZ 6

1. *Tu dois* —— (have) *faim.*

    a. être
    b. avoir
    c. bon

2. *Pas de* —— (butter).

    a. bon
    b. beurre
    c. bonne

3. —— (there is) *un bon restaurant à l'hotel.*

    a. il y a
    b. il va
    c. c'est

4. *Mon café est* —— (cold).

    a. froid
    b. chaud
    c. chose

5. *Donnez-moi la* ——— (same) *chose.*

a. aussi
b. même
c. beurre

6. *Garçon une* ——— (napkin) *s'il vous plaît.*

a. fourchette
b. couteau
c. serviette

7. *Voulez-vous* ——— (also) *me donner une fourchette?*

a. bien
b. pas
c. aussi

8. *Garçon,* ——— (the check).

a. la fois
b. le garçon
c. l'addition

9. *Un peu* ——— (more) *de sucre.*

a. plaît
b. nous
c. plus

10. *Gardez la* ——— (change).

a. beaucoup
b. monnaie
c. laissez

ANSWERS

1—b; 2—b; 3—a; 4—a; 5—b; 6—c; 7—c; 8—c; 9—c; 10—b.

LESSON 38

80. IN, ON, UNDER

1. *dans* "in, into"

C'est dans le dictionnaire.	It's in the dictionary.
Il l'a mis dans sa poche.	He put it into his pocket.
Vous le trouverez dans sa chambre.	You'll find it in his room.
J'ai quelque chose dans l'oeil.	I have something in my eye.
Mettez-le dans le tiroir.	Put it into the drawer.
Je serai là dans un instant.	I'll be there in a minute.

2. *dedans* "inside"

Regardez dans le dictionnaire, c'est dedans.	Look in the dictionary; you'll find it there.
Regardez là-dedans.	Look in there.

3. *en* "in"

En means "in" in certain expressions:[1]

En avril.	In April.
En été.	In the summer.
En ville.	In town.
En une seconde.	In a second. In a jiffy.

4. *sur* "on"

Mettez cette lettre sur son bureau.	Put this letter on his desk.
Son nom est sur la porte.	His name is on the door.
Ecrivez-le sur l'enveloppe.	Write it on the envelope.
Vous pouvez compter sur moi.	You can count on me.

[1] See page 135 for other meanings.

5. *sous* "under"

C'est sous la chaise. — It's under the chair.
Vous trouverez ce livre sous les outres. — You'll find the book under the others.
Il l'a mis sous le lit. — He put it under the bed.
Je l'ai trouvé sous un tas de papiers. — I found it under a pile of papers.

6. *dessus* "on, on top of"

Mettez-le au-dessus. — Put it on top.
Regardez donc dessus. — Look on the top.
Mettez ce livre là-dessus. — Put the book on that.

7. *dessous* "under, underneath"

Mettez-ça dessous. — Put that underneath.
Voyez ci-dessous. — Look under here.

8. *si* "if"
Si becomes *s'* before *il* or *ils*.

Si je peux. — If I can.
Si j'ai de l'argent. — If I have (enough) money.
S'il vient. — If he comes.
Si vous voulez. — If you wish.
S'il vous plaît. — Please. ("If it pleases you.")
Si ça vous plaît. — If you like that.

9. *si* "so"
Unlike *si* meaning "if," *si* meaning "so" never becomes *s'*.

C'est si bon — It's so good!
C'est si commode! — It's so convenient!

Il se fait si tard!	It's so late.
Ce n'est pas si mauvais que ça.	It's not as bad as that.
Il n'est pas si ignorant que ça.	He's not as ignorant as that.

10. *par* "by"

Par où?	Which way?
Par ici.	This way.
Par là.	Tha way.
Par lui.	By him.
Par example.	For example.
Parfois.	Sometimes.

11. *sans* "without"

Sans moi.	Without me.
Sans argent.	Without money.
Sans rien.	Without anything.
Sand personne.	Without anyone.
Sans faute.	Without fail.
Sans difficulté.	Without difficulty.
Vous pouvez le faire sans aucune difficulté.	You can do it without any difficulty.

QUIZ 27

1. *Mettez ça dessous.*
2. *Par où?*
3. *C'est dans le dictionnaire.*
4. *Ecrivez-le sur l'enveloppe.*
5. *Son nom est sur la porte.*
6. *Regardez donc dessus.*
7. *Si ça vous plaît.*
8. *Ce n'est pas si mauvais que ça.*
9. *Parfois.*

10. *Sans faute.*
11. *Sans difficulté.*
12. *Sans argent.*
13. *Si vous voulez.*
14. *Mettez-le au-dessus.*
15. *Vous trouverez ce livre sous les autres.*

1. It's in the dictionary.
2. Put that underneath.
3. Which way?
4. His name is on the door.
5. Write it on the envelope.
6. You'll find the book under the others.
7. Put it on top.
8. Look on the top.
9. If you wish.
10. If you like that.
11. It's not as bad as that.
12. Sometimes.
13. Without money.
14. Without fail.
15. Without difficulty.

ANSWERS

1—2; 2—3; 3—1; 4—5; 5—4; 6—8; 7—10; 8—11; 9—12; 10—14; 11—15; 12—13; 13—9; 14—7; 15—6.

REVIEW QUIZ 7

1. *Je préfère* —— (that one).

    a. ce
    b. celui-là
    c. cette

2. *Que veut dire* —— (this)?

    a. ceci
    b. cela
    c. cet

3. *Je ne sais pas* —— (how).

    a. encore
    b. souvent
    c. comment

4. *Il ne vient* —— (never).

    a. quand
    b. jamais
    c. comment

5. *Il n'a* —— (nothing) *dit.*

    a. plus
    b. quand
    c. rien

6. *Votre livre est meilleur que le* —— (his).

    a. vôtres
    b. lui
    c. sien

7. *Je suis* —— (happy) *de faire votre connaissance.*

    a. heureux
    b. présenter
    c. connaissance

8. *A la* ——— (week) *prochaine.*

a. vrai
b. semaine
c. fois

9. *A la* ——— (next) *fois.*

a. nouvelles
b. prochaine
c. jours

10. *Ça va bien,* ——— (thanks).

a. neuf
b. merci
c. comment

11. *Téléphonez-moi un de ces* ——— (days).

a. semaine
b. jours
c. neuf

12. *Est-ce que vous* ——— (know) *mon ami?*

a. connaissez
b. recontrez
c. pense

13. *Non, je ne* ——— (think) *pas.*

a. plaisir
b. pense
c. connais

14. *J'* ——— (hope) *vous revoir bientôt.*

a. enchanté
b. fait
c. espère

15. *Je vais vous l'* —— (write).

a. avez
b. écrire
c. retrouvons

16. *Vous pouvez m'appeler le* —— (morning).

a. numéro
b. adresse
c. matin

17. *Enchanté de vous avoir* —— (met).

a. enchanté
b. recontré
c. fait

18. —— (give) *-moi votre adresse personnelle.*

a. vais
b. donnez
c. appeler

19. *C'est très* —— (good).

a. bien
b. bientôt
c. aussi

20. *A* —— (soon).

a. bientôt
b. matin
c. adresse

ANSWERS

1—b; 2—a; 3—c; 4—b; 5—c; 6—c; 7—a; 8—b; 9—b; 10—b; 11—b; 12—a; 13—b; 14—c; 15—b; 16—c; 17—b; 18—b; 19—a; 20—a.

81. APARTMENT HUNTING

(Apartment Hunting)

1. **Je viens pour l'appartement.**
   I've come about the apartment.
2. **Lequel?**
   Which one?
3. **Celui qui est à louer.**
   The one for rent.
4. **Mais il y en a deux.**
   But there are two.
5. **Puis-je avoir des détails?**
   Can you describe them?
6. **Celui du cinquième est non-meublé.**
   The one on the fifth floor is unfurnished.
7. **Et l'autre?**
   And the other?
8. **L'appartement du deuxième est meublé.**
   The one on the second floor is furnished.
9. **Combien de pièces ont-ils chacun?**
   How many rooms does each one have?
10. **Celui du cinquième a quatre pièces, cuisine et salle de bain.**
    The one on the fifth floor has four rooms, a kitchen and bath.
11. **Donne-t-il sur la cour?**
    Does it face the court?
12. **Non, sur la rue.**
    No, the street.
13. **Et celui du second?**
    And how about the one on the second floor?

14. **Il a cinq pièces, trois chambres à coucher, une salle à manger et un salon.**
It has five rooms, three bedrooms, a dining room and a parlor.

15. **Est-il sur la cour aussi?**
Is it also on a court?

16. **Non, sur la rue.**
No, it faces the street.

17. **Quel est le prix du loyer?**
What's the rent?

18. **Le grand est de dix mille plus les charges.**
The larger one is ten thousand francs plus extras.

19. **Et celui qui est meublé?**
And the furnished one?

20. **Quatorze mille plus les charges.**
That's fourteen thousand francs plus extras.

21. **De quel genre et dans quel état sont les meubles?**
What kind of furniture does it have? Is it in good condition?

22. **C'est un mobilier ancien en excellent état.**
It's antique furniture (and) in excellent condition.

23. **Le linge et l'argenterie sont-ils compris?**
Are linens and silverware included?

24. **Il y a tout ce qu'il faut, même la batterie de cuisine.**
You'll find everything you need, even a complete set of kitchen utensils.

25. **Le propriétaire fait-il un bail et de quelle durée?**
Would the owner give me a lease? (And) For how long?

26. **Il faudrait voir le gérant.**
You'd have to see the renting agent for that.

27. **Quelles sont les conditions?**
What are the terms?

28. **On paye trois mois d'avance.**
You pay three months' rent in advance.

29. **Rien d'autre?**
Nothing else?

30. **Et de références, bien entendu!**
References, of course.

31. **Au fait, y a-t-il un ascenseur?**
By the way, is there an elevator?

32. **Non, il n'y en a pas.**
No, there isn't.

33. **Ah, c'est dommage!**
That's too bad.

34. **A part ça, la maison est très moderne, vous savez.**
Apart from that, though, the house is quite modern.

35. **Comment ça?**
What do you mean?

36. **Il y a le chauffage central, escalier de service.**
There's central heating and a back stairway.

37. **Y a-t-il l'eau courante, chaude et froide?**
Is there hot and cold running water?

38. **Certainement. Les salles de bain ont été refaites récemment.**
Of course. The bathrooms were remodeled recently.

39. **Y a-t-il des placards?**
Are there any closets?

40. **Oui, énormes et nombreux.**
Yes, lots of large ones.

41. **J'oubliais, y a-t-il des chambres de domestiques?**
I forgot—are there servants' quarters?
42. **Mais oui, elles sont chauffées et elles ont l'électricité.**
Yes, they're heated and they have electricity.
43. **Peut-on visiter?**
Can one see the place?
44. **Seulement dans la matinée.**
Only in the morning.
45. **C'est bien, je reviendrai demain matin. Merci beaucoup.**
Very well, I'll come tomorrow morning. Thanks a lot.
46. **De rien, à votre service.**
Not at all. Glad to be able to help you.

NOTES

Title: *A la recherche d'un appartement.* "In search of an apartment."

1. *Je viens pour* "I come for."
3. *Celui qui est* "the one which is."
4. Notice the use of *en* ("of it, of them"). See page 135.
5. "May (can) I have some details?"
9. *Chacun* each, each one. *Ont-ils chacun?* "do they each have?"
11. *Donne-t-il.* For the *t*, see page 31.—*Donner sur* to face out on.
13. *Second* second. In this word the *c* is pronounced as though it were written *g*. You can also say *le deuxième étage* the second floor.
14. *Chambre à coucher* ("room for sleeping") bedroom.—*Salle à manger* ("room for eating") dining room.—*Le salon* living room,

parlor.

17. *Quel est le prix du loyer? A quel est le montant* ("amount") *du loyer? Loyer* rent. *Louer* to rent.
18. *Plus les charges* plus the extras. "Extras" refer not to gas or electricity (paid by the tenant directly to the company) but to things like city taxes, garbage removal, etc. Some landlords charge a fixed percentage of the rent (ten percent, say) for these extras.
21. *Genre* class, kind. *De quel genre* what style. *Etat* state, condition.
22. *C'est un mobilier ancien.* It's antique furniture.
23. *Argenterie* silverware. *Argent* silver. *Sont-ils compris?* Are they included? *Compris* ("included") is from *comprendre* to include; also to understand.
24. *Tout ce qu'il faut* everything that's needed. Notice the *que* before *il* becomes *qu'il* (see page 152).
25. *Propriétaire* owner; here it means "landlord." *Durée* duration, length of time.
26. *Gérant* manager (also hotel manager). The *gérant* of an apartment house is the agent who manages a building and who receives a certain percentage of the income.
27. Apartments in France are rented on a yearly basis, the rent being paid every three months. It is customary for a tenant to leave a deposit for three or six months' rent which is applied to the last three or six months of the lease.—*Un bail,* unlike our lease, is usually for three, six or nine years.
31. *Au fait* by the way, incidentally. *Il y a-t-il* = *Est-ce qu'il y a.*
32. Notice the use of *en* (see page 135).

34. Notice this use of *vous savez* ("you know").
35. *Comment ça?* ("How's that?") How come? What do you mean?
36. *Escalier de service* "service stairway."
37. *Courant* running; from *courir* to run. The feminine form *(courante)* is used here because it refers to *l'eau* which is feminine.
38. *Refaites* is from *refaire*. It is feminine plural because it refers to the feminine plural noun, *les salles*.
40. *Enorme* large, enormous. *Nombreux* numerous.
41. *J'oubliais* I forgot. *Chambres de domestiques* "Rooms for the servants." *Les domestiques* the servants. The last floor of an apartment house usually has quarters for the maids.
43. *Peut-on visiter?* "Can one visit?"
44. *Matin* is the general word for "morning." When you say "in the morning," etc. you use *matinée: dans la matinée* in the morning.
45. *Je reviendrai* I'll return, I'll come back; from *revenir* to return.
46. *De rien* ("Of nothing") is one reply to *merci*. Another common reply is *Il n'y a pas de quoi*. "There is no reason to thank me."—*A votre service* "at your service."

QUIZ 28

1. —— (how many) *de pièces ont-ils?*
a. autre
b. combien
c. chacun

2. *Donne-t-il sur la* —— (street)?

   a. cour
   b. salon
   c. rue

3. *Quel est le* —— (price) *du loyer?*

   a. prix
   b. mille
   c. genre

4. *On* —— (pay) *trois mois à l'avance.*

   a. sont
   b. entendu
   c. paye

5. *La* —— (house) *est très moderne.*

   a. dommage
   b. maison
   c. comment

6. *Il y a l'eau courante* —— (warm) *et froide.*

   a. chaude
   b. salles
   c. bain

7. *Y a-t-il des* —— (rooms) *de domestiques?*

   a. nombreux
   b. chambres
   c. énormes

8. —— (only) *dans la matinée.*

   a. visiter
   b. seulement
   c. chauffées

9. *Je reviendrai* —— (tomorrow) *matin.*

   a. demain
   b. seulement
   c. bien

10. —— (thank you) *beaucoup.*

a. matin
b. service
c. merci

ANSWERS

1—b; 2—c; 3—a; 4—c; 5—b; 6—a; 7—b; 8—b; 9—a; 10—c.

LESSON 39

82. TO COME, TO SAY, TO DO

1. *Venir* to come

je viens	I come	*nous venons*	we come
tu viens	you come	*vous venez*	you come
il vient	he comes	*ils viennent*	they come

Viens	Come! *(fam.)*
Venez!	Come!
Venez ici.	Come here.
Venez avec moi.	Come with me.
Venez encore.	Come again.
Venez à la maison	Come to the house.
Venez un soir	Come some evening.
Ne venez pas.	Don't come.
D'où venez-vous?	Where are you coming from?
Je viens de paris.	I'm coming from Paris. I come from Paris.
Je viens du théâtre.	I'm coming from the theatre.
Je viens tout de suite.	I'm coming right away.

Venir de . . . means "to have just."

Je viens de le voir.	I've just seen him.
Je viens de sortir de chez lui.	I've just left his place (his house).
Je viens de le faire.	I've just done it.

2. *Dire* to say

je dis	I say	*nous disons*	we say
tu dis	you say	*vous dites*	you say
il dit	he says	*ils disent*	they say

On dit que. . . .	It's said that. . . . People say that. . . . They say that. . . .
On m'a dit.	I've been told.
C'est à dire. . . .	That's to say. . . . That is. . . .
C'est difficile à dire.	It's hard to say.
Dites!	Say (it)! Tell (it)!
Dites-le.	Say it.
Dites-le encore.	Say it again.
Dites-le en français.	Say it in French.
Dites-le lentement.	Say it slowly.
Ne le dites pas.	Don't say it.
Ne dites pas ça.	Don't say that.
Dites donc.	Tell me. Well, tell me. Say. . . .
Dites donc, vous n'êtes pas sèrieux, n'est-ce pas?	Say, you're not serious, are you?
Dites-moi.	Tell me.
Dites-le moi	Say it to me. Tell me it.
Dites-lui.	Tell him.
Dites-le-lui.	Tell it to him.
Dites-lui de venir.	Tell him to come.
Ne le lui dites pas.	Don't tell it to him. Don't tell him.
Ne lui dites rien.	Don't tell him anything.

Surtout ne le dites à personne.	Above all, don't tell it to anybody.
Qu'est-ce que vous dites?	What did you say? ("What is it that you say?")
Pouvez-vous me dire où se trouve l'hôtel?	Can you tell me where there's a hotel?
Qu'est-ce que vous voulez dire?	What do you mean? ("What do you want to say?")
Il n'a rien dit.	He hasn't said anything.

QUIZ 29

1. *Je viens du théatre.*	1. Come with me.
2. *Je viens de le faire.*	2. Where are you coming from?
3. *Je viens tout de suite.*	3. Come some evening.
4. *D'où venez-vous?*	4. I'm coming right away.
5. *Dites-moi.*	5. I'm coming from the theatre.
6. *Dites le en français.*	6. Say it in French.
7. *C'est difficile à dire.*	7. That's to say. . . .
8. *Venez un soir.*	8. It's hard to say.
9. *Venez avec moi.*	9. I've just done it.
10. *C'est à dire. . . .*	10. Tell me.

ANSWERS

1—5; 2—9; 3—4; 4—2; 5—10; 6—6; 7—8; 8—3; 9—1; 10—7.

3. *Faire* to do

je fais	I do	*nous faisons*	we do
tu fais	you do	*vous faites*	you do
il fait	he does	*ils font*	they do

Je le fais.	I do it. I'm doing it.
Je ne le fais pas.	I don't do it. I'm not doing it.
Que faites-vous? / *Qu'est-ce que vous faites?*	What are you doing?
Comment faites-vous ça?	How do you do that?
Qu'est-ce que vous avez fait?	What have you been doing?
Ne le faites pas.	Don't do it!
Ne le faites plus.	Don't do it anymore.
C'est fait.	It's done. It's over.
Deux et deux font quatre.	Two and two are four.
C'est différent.	That makes a difference.
Ça me fait mal.	That hurts me.
Je ne fais rien.	I'm not doing anything.
Ça ne fait rien.	That doesn't matter. I don't mind.
Ça ne fait rien du tout.	It doesn't matter at all.
Ça ne me fait rien.	It doesn't matter to me.
Faites cela (ça)!	Do that.
Ne faites pas cela (ça)!	Don't do it!
Faites-le encore!	Do it again.
Faites-le encore une fois!	Do it once more.
Faites ça vite!	Do it quickly!
Ne faites pas cela (ça)!	Don't do that!
Ne faites rein.	Don't do anything.

Faites attention!	Pay attention!
Faites donc attention.	Mind what you're doing.
Faites bien attention.	Pay close attention.
Ne faites pas attention à cela (ça).	Don't mind that. Don't pay attention to that.
Ne faites pas attention à lui.	Don't mind him. Don't pay any attention to him.
Il ne faut pas faire cela (ça).	You (we, etc.) mustn't do that. That mustn't be done.
Je viens de le faire.	I've just done it.
J'ai déjà fait sa connaissance.	I've already met him. ("I've already made his acquaintance.")
Il fait froid.	It's cold. The weather's cold.
Il fait chaud.	It's hot. The weather's hot.
Vous permettez?—Faites donc! Je vous en prie.	May I? Please do! Go ahead
Que faire?	What's to be done? What shall we do? What can be done? ("What to do?").
Comment faire?	How shall we do it? What shall we do? ("How to do?")
Qui a fait cela (ça)?	Who did that?
Je ne sais que faire.	I don't know what to do.

QUIZ 30

1. *Qu'est-ce que vous avez fait?*	1. Do that!

2. *Ne le faites pas.*	2. Do it quickly.
3. *C'est fait.*	3. What are you doing?
4. *Ça ne fait rien.*	4. What have you done?
5. *Il fait froid.*	5. Don't do it.
6. *Faites donc attention.*	6. It's done. It's over.
7. *Faites-le encore une fois.*	7. That makes a difference.
8. *Qui a fait ça?*	8. Never mind. That doesn't matter.
9. *Je viens de le faire.*	9. It doesn't matter at all.
10. *Faites attention!*	10. Do it once more. ("One more time.")
11. *C'est different.*	11. Pay attention! Mind what you're doing.
12. *Faites ça!*	12. Pay attention! Mind what you're doing.
13. *Qu'est-ce que vous faites?*	13. I've just done it.
14. *Faites ça vite.*	14. It's cold.
15. *Ça ne fait rien du tout.*	15. Who did that?

ANSWERS

1—4; 2—5; 3—6; 4—8; 5—14; 6—11; 7—10; 8—15; 9—13; 10—12; 11—7; 12—1; 13—3; 14—2; 15—9.

WORD STUDY

capable	capable
la chance	chance
la créature	creature
la direction	direction
la leçon	lesson
le papier	paper
sérieux	serious
sévère	severe
la terme	term
l'usage (m.)	usage

REVIEW QUIZ 8

1. *Je* —— (I'm coming) *tout de suite.*

   a. venez
   b. viens
   c. vois

2. *C'est difficile à* —— (say).

   a. venir
   b. venez
   c. dire

3. *Qu'est ce que vous* —— (do)?

   a. dire
   b. faites
   c. dites

4. *Je ne sais que* —— (do).

   a. dire
   b. venir
   c. faire

5. *Quand j'habitais en France, j'* —— (had) *beaucoup d'amis français.*

   a. *étais*
   b. *avais*
   c. *faisais*

6. *Ne le* —— (take) *pas.*

   a. *prenez*
   b. *envoyez*
   c. *essayez*

7. —— (stop) *tout de suite.*

   a. *arrêtez*
   b. *apportez*
   c. *aidez*

8. *Je termine en* —— (hoping) *bientôt recevoir de vos nouvelles.*

   a. *revenant*
   b. *espérant*
   c. *habitant*

9. *Je ne* —— (see) *pas.*

   a. *voyons*
   b. *savoir*
   c. *vois*

10. *Venez nous* —— (see) *un soir.*

    a. *voir*
    b. *sais*
    c. *vu*

11. *Il n'en* —— (knows) *pas davantage.*

    a. *vois*
    b. *sait*
    c. *savoir*

12. *Il a oublié tout ce qu'il* —— (knew).

a. savait
b. savez
c. pouvez

13. *Il* —— (holds, is holding) *son chapeau à la main.*

a. tenez
b. peut
c. tient

14. *Je ne vois pas comment il* —— (can) *faire cela.*

a. tient
b. peut
c. puis

15. *Il ne* —— (understand) *pas.*

a. pouvez
b. comprend
c. mettre

16. —— (put) *votre chapeau.*

a. comprend
b. mettez
c. mis

17. *Je ne* —— (know) *personne dans cette ville.*

a. suivre
b. voulez
c. connais

18. *Il* —— (wants) *revenir.*

a. voulez
b. connaît
c. veut

19. Vous ne me —— (owe) *rien.*

a. devez
b. demander
c. attend

20. Il ne —— (ask) *rien.*

a. attendre
b. demande
c. doit

ANSWERS

1—b; 2—c; 3—b; 4—c; 5—b; 6—a; 7—a; 8—b; 9—c; 10—a; 11—b; 12—a; 13—c; 14—b; 15—b; 16—b; 17—c; 18—c; 19—a; 20—b.

83. I'M A STRANGER HERE

(I'm a Stranger Here)

Je ne suis pas d'ici.
I'm not from here.

1. **Pardon, Monsieur.**
   I beg your pardon, sir.

2. **Je vous en prie.**
   Not at all.

3. **Pourriez-vous me donner quelques renseignements?**
   Could you give me some information?

4. **Certainement, avec plaisir.**
   Certainly! I'd be glad to.

5. **Je ne connais pas la ville, je ne m'y retrouve pas.**
   I don't know the town, I can't find my way about.

6. **C'est pourtant bien simple.**
   It's quite simple.

7. **C'est que je ne suis pas d'ici.**
   You see, I'm a stranger here.

8. **Ça ne fait rien.**
   That's not too serious.

9. **Mais si, il faut tout m'expliquer.**
   But it is, because it's necessary to explain everything to me.

10. **Alors, écoutez-moi.**
    Then, listen to me.

11. **Je vous écoute, monsieur.**
    I'm listening.

12. **Commençons par la poste.**
    Let's begin with the post office.

13. **C'est ça. C'est une bonne idée!**
    Fine! That's a good idea.

14. **Voyez-vous la maison du coin?**
    You see the building on the corner?

15. **Celle avec une lanterne bleue?**
    The one with the blue lantern?

16. **Oui, c'est bien ça, la poste est au rez-de-chaussée.**
    Yes, that's the one. The post office is on the ground floor.

17. **La boutique avec un drapeau, qu'est-ce que c'est.**
    The store with the flag—what's that?

18. **La commissariat de police.**
    That's the police station.

19. **Il y a encore une autre maison avec un drapeau.**
There's another building with a flag.

20. **C'est la mairie.**
That's the City Hall.

21. **Je vois. Et quel est le nom de cette rue?**
I see. (And) What's the name of this street?

22. **La rue de la Préfecture. Voyez-vous cette boutique?**
Prefecture Street. Do you see that store?

23. **Laquelle? A droite?**
Which one? The one on the right?

24. **Oui. Avec un grand globe vert dans la vitrine.**
Yes. The one with a large green globe in the window.

25. **Et un rouge dans l'autre?**
And the red one in the other?

26. **C'est ça. Eh bien, c'est la pharmacie.**
That's right. Well, that's the pharmacy.

27. **Ah, très bien.**
I see. ("Very well.")

28. **Le docteur habite tout à côté.**
The doctor lives right next door.

29. **Est-ce un bon médecin?**
Is he a good doctor?

30. **Excellent, il est tous les matins à l'hôpital.**
An excellent one. He's at the hospital every morning.

31. **Où se trouve l'hôpital?**
Where's the hospital?

32. **Dans la deuxième rue à gauche, avant d'arriver à la Route Nationale.**
Two blocks from here, to your left, just before you come to the main highway.

33. **Y a-t-il une papeterie ici?**
Is there a stationery store here?

34. **Bien sûr, tout à côté, dans la Grande Rue, là où se trouve votre hôtel.**
Of course. (It's) not far from here, on Main Street, where your hotel is.

35. **Maintenant j'y suis.**
Now I understand everything.

36. **Pourquoi n'acheteriez-vous pas un plan?**
Why don't you buy a guide book?

37. **C'est une bonne idée! Où puis-je en trouver?**
That's a good idea. Where can I find one?

38. **A la gare, ou bien au kiosque à journaux.**
Either at the station or at the newspaper stand.

39. **Où se trouve la gare?**
Where's the station?

40. **La gare est à l'autre extrémité de la rue de la Préfecture.**
The station is at the other end of Prefecture Street.

41. **Où se trouve le kiosque à journaux?**
And where's there a newspaper stand?

42. **Au coin de la rue.**
On the corner.

43. **Merci beaucoup.**
Thank you very much.

44. **Ne me remerciez pas, c'est la moindre des choses.**
Not at all.

45. J'ai eu de la chance de vous rencontrer. Vous paraissez bien connaître la ville.
I was lucky to meet you. You seem to know the town very well.

46. C'est bien naturel, je suis le maire de la ville.
It's quite natural. I'm the mayor ("of the town").

NOTES

Title: *Je ne suis pas d'ici.* "I'm not from here."

1. *Pardon* (or *Je vous demande pardon.)* is used when you ask for something, when you pass in front of someone, etc. The reply is *Je vous en prie.—Excuse me* is *Excusez-moi,* the reply to which is *Faites!* or *Faites donc!* (Do! Please do! Go ahead! etc.)

3. *Pourriez-vous* could you; from *pouvoir* to be able (see page 251). Another way of saying this is: *Voulez-vous être assez aimable de me donner quelques renseignements?* ("Would you be kind enough to give me . . . ?")—*Renseignements* information. (Notice the plural form in French.) *Bureau de renseignements* ("Office of Information") Information (Bureau).

4. *Avec plaisir.* "With pleasure."

5. *Connaître* to be acquainted with (see page 254)—*Retrouver* to find again.

7. *C'est que* . . . "It's that . . ." Here it means: "The reason is . . ." "It's because . . ."

8. *Ça ne fait rien.* "It doesn't matter." = *Ça n'a pas d'importance.* "That has no importance." Both expressions can often be translated "Never mind," "Not at all," "That's nothing," "That's all right."

9. *Mais si.* "but yes." *Si* is used when denying a previous statement.

10. *Ecoutez-moi* ("Listen to me") and *Je vous écoute* ("I'm listening") are often used in French when one person begins to explain something and the other person tells him to go ahead.

12. *La poste = Le bureau de poste; Commençons.* Let's begin.

13. *C'est ça.* "That's it." This is one of the commonest French expressions. It can be translated in many ways: "That's right," "Good!" "Fine!" "All right!" "O. K.," etc.

15. *La lanterne bleue* the blue lantern. Post offices in Paris have blue lamps outside. —*Celle* is feminine because it refers to *la maison*.

16. Post offices in Paris are located in private buildings. In small towns the post office is located in a separate building where the postmaster lives. Mailman is *facteur.—Rez-de-chaussée* ground floor. *Entresol* the floor above the ground floor, a kind of mezzanine. In France the first floor is the one which comes after the *rez-de-chaussée* or, in a building which has an *entresol*, the one

which comes after the *entresol*.

20. *La mairie* City Hall. There is a *mairie* in every French *commune* and one in each *arrondissement* of Paris. The Mayor is *le Maire*, his assistant is *l'Adjoint au Maire*. They are addressed as *Monsieur le Maire*.

21. *Je vois*. I see; from *voir* to see.

22. "The street of the Préfecture."

26. *C'est ça*. See Note 13 above.—*Eh bien* is very common. It can often be translated "Well," "Well now," "So," etc.

27. Notice this use of *très bien*.

28. Physicians are called *docteurs* or *médecins* and are addressed as *docteur*.

30. *Tous les matins* ("all the mornings") every morning.

31. "Where does it find itself?" *Trouver* to find.

32. *Avant d'arriver* before coming to.

35. *Maintenant j'y suis*. ("Now I'm there.") Now I understand. Now I get it. Oh, now I see!

36. *Achèteriez*. Conditional form of *acheter* to buy.

38. *Kiosque à journaux* newspaper stand.

40. *L'autre extrémité* the other end.

42. "At the corner of the street."

44. *Ne me remerciez pas*. "Don't thank me."—*C'est la moindre des choses*. ("It's the least of things.") It's nothing. = *Il n'y a pas de quoi* ("There's nothing to thank me for.") Not at all.

QUIZ 31

1. —— (not at all).

   a. *je vous en prie*
   b. *il n'y a pas de quoi*
   c. *de rien*

2. *Pourriez-vous me* —— (give) *quelques renseignements?*

   a. *plaisir*
   b. *mais*
   c. *donner*

3. *Il faut tout m'* —— (explain).

   a. *écouter*
   b. *expliquer*
   c. *commençons*

4. *Voyez-vous la* —— (house) *du coin?*

   a. *maison*
   b. *poste*
   c. *lanterne*

5. *Quel est le nom de cette* —— (street)?

   a. *bien*
   b. *rue*
   c. *coin*

6. *Le docteur* —— (lives) *tout à côté.*

   a. *habite*
   b. *tombe*
   c. *fait*

7. *Avec un grand globe* —— (green).

   a. *rouge*
   b. *vert*
   c. *vitrine*

8. *Il est tous les* —— (mornings) *à l'hôpital.*

   a. *médecin*
   b. *matins*
   c. *trouve*

9. *J'ai eu de la* —— (luck) *de vous rencontrer.*
   a. *merci*
   b. *coin*
   c. *chance*

10. *Où se trouve* —— (the station)?
   a. *la poste*
   b. *la gare*
   c. *la maison*

ANSWERS

1—c; 2—c; 3—b; 4—a; 5—b; 6—a; 7—b; 8—b; 9—c; 10—b.

LESSON 40

84. THE COMMONEST VERB FORMS

1. I Finish and I Take

I Finish		I Take	
je finis	*nous finissons*	*je prends*	*nous prenons*
tu finis	*vous finissez*	*tu prends*	*vous prenez*
il finit	*ils finissent*	*il prend*	*ils prennent*

Compare these forms:

Donner to give	*Finir* to finish	*Prendre* to take
je donne	*je finis*	*je prends*
tu donnes	*tu finis*	*tu prends*
il donne	*il finit*	*il prend*
nous donnons	*nous finissons*	*nous prenons*
vous donnez	*vous finissez*	*vous prenez*
ils donnent	*ils finissent*	*ils prennent*

Verbs ending in *-er* (the vast majority) are like *donner* in the present.

Verbs ending in *-ir* are like *finir* in the present.

Other Examples:

obéir	to obey
choisir	to choose
réussir	to succeed
fournir	to furnish

Verbs ending in *-re* are like *prendre* in the present:

Other Examples:

vendre	to sell
répondre	to answer
perdre	to lose

Verbs ending in *-oir* have the following forms in the present:

Recevoir to receive

je reçois	*nous recevons*
tu reçois	*vous recevez*
il reçoit	*ils reçoivent*

2. I Shall Give, Finish, Take

Donner to give	*Finir* to finish	*Prendre* to take
je donnerai	*je finirai*	*je prendrai*
tu donneras	*tu finiras*	*tu prendras*
il donnera	*il finira*	*il prendra*
nous donnerons	*nous finirons*	*nous prendrons*
vous donnerez	*vous finirez*	*vous prendrez*
ils donneront	*ils finiront*	*ils prendront*

a. Notice that to form the future you add the following endings to the stem *(donner-, finir-, prendr-):*

je —ai	*nous —ons*
tu —as	*vous —ez*
il —a	*ils —ont*

b. Some Irregular Futures:

I Shall Be

je serai	*nous serons*
tu seras	*vous serez*
il sera	*ils seront*

I Shall Have

j'aurai	*nous aurons*
tu auras	*vous aurez*
il aura	*il auront*

I Shall Make or Do

je ferai	*nous ferons*
tu feras	*vous ferez*
il fera	*ils feront*

I Shall Say

je dirai	*nous dirons*
tu diras	*vous direz*
il dira	*ils diront*

I Shall Go

j'irai	*nous irons*
tu iras	*vous irez*
il ira	*ils iront*

j'écrirai	I shall write
je viendrai	I shall come
je verrai	I shall see
je tiendrai	I shall have *or* hold
je voudrai	I shall want *or* wish
je recevrai	I shall receive
je mettrai	I shall put
je pourrai	I shall be able
je saurai	I shall know
je devrai	I shall owe *or* have to
Il faudra que . . .	It will be necessary to . . .

3. I Was, I Had, I Did

I Was, I Used to Be

j'étais	*nous étions*
tu étais	*vous étiez*
il était	*ils étaient*

I Had, I Used to Have

j'avais	*nous avions*
tu avais	*vous aviez*
il avait	*ils avaient*

I Did, I Used to Do

je faisais	*nous faisions*
tu faisais	*vous faisiez*
il faisait	*ils faisaient*

Imperfect Tense

je —ais	*nous —ions*
tu —ais	*vous —iez*
il —ait	*ils —aient*

These forms make up the "imperfect tense" which expresses continuous or repeated action in the past.

Quand j'habitais en France, j'avais beaucoup d'amis français.	When I lived (was living) in France, I had (used to have) many French friends.

4. I Have Given, Spoken, etc.

I Have Given

j'ai donné	*nous avons donné*
tu as donné	*vous avez donné*
il a donné	*ils ont donné*

I Have Spoken

j'ai parlé	*nous avons parlé*
tu as parlé	*vous avez parlé*
il a parlé	*ils ont parlé*

Other Examples:

j'ai apporté	I have brought
j'ai envoyé	I have sent
j'ai acheté	I have bought

The forms *donner* "to give," *parler* "to speak," *demander* "to ask" are called "the infinitive."

The forms *donné, parlé, demandé,* etc. are called "the past participle."

donner	to give	*donné*	given
parler	to speak	*parlé*	spoken
demander	to ask	*demandé*	asked

The form *j'ai,* etc., plus the past participle (called "the past indefinite tense") is used when you refer to some single event that took place in the past.

Je lui ai donné de l'argent. I gave him some money.

This tense can usually be translated by the English past ("I gave"). Sometimes, however, it is used where we could use the past perfect ("I have given").

Here are some examples of past participles formed from other types of verbs.

Verbs ending in *-ir:*

finir	to finish	*fini*	finished

Verbs ending in *-re:*

répondre	to answer	*répondu*	answered
descendre	to go down	*descendu*	gone down
vendre	to sell	*vendu*	sold

Verbs ending in *-oir:*

recevoir	to receive	*reçu*	received
voir	to see	*vu*	seen
pouvoir	to be able	*pu*	been able
savoir	to know	*su*	known

5. I Have Been, Have Had, Etc.

I Have Been

j'ai été	*nous avons été*
tu as été	*vous avez été*
il a été	*ils ont été*

I Have Had

j'ai eu	*nous avons eu*
tu as eu	*vous avez eu*
il a eu	*ils ont eu*

I Have Done or Made

j'ai fait	*nous avons fait*
tu as fait	*vous avez fait*
il a fait	*ils ont fait*

I Have Said

j'ai dit	*nous avons dit*
tu as dit	*vous avez dit*
il a dit	*ils ont dit*

Notice the form or the past participle of these verbs:

être	to be	*été*	been
faire	to do	*fait*	done
dire	to say	*dit*	said
avoir	to have	*eu*	had
voir	to see	*vu*	seen
savoir	to know	*su*	known

6. I Have Gone, Etc.

I Have Gone

je suis allé	*nous sommes allés*
tu es allé	*vous êtes allés*
il est allé	*ils sont allés*

Compare: *j'ai donné* "I have given" and *je suis allé* "I have gone."

Notice that most verbs have *j'ai, tu as, il a,* etc., but that a few (chiefly verbs of motion) have *je suis, tu es, il est,* etc.

The commonest verbs which have the latter form are:

je suis entré	I have entered, I entered
je suis sorti	I have gone out, I went out
je suis arrivé	I have arrived, I arrived
je suis parti	I have left, I left
je suis monté	I have gone up, I went up
je suis descendu	I have gone down, I went down
je suis resté	I have remained, I remained
je suis revenu	I have returned, I returned
je suis tombé	I have fallen, I fell
je suis né	I was born
je suis devenu	I have become, I became

7. I Had Given, Gone, Etc.

I Had Given

j'avais donné	*nous avions donné*
tu avais donné	*vous aviez donné*
il avait donné	*ils avaient donné*

Other Examples:

j'avais parlé	I had spoken
j'avais demandé	I had asked
j'avais apporté	I had brought

I Had Gone

j'étais allé	*nous étions allés*
tu étais allé	*vous étiez allés*
il était allé	*ils étaient allés*

Other Examples:

j'étais arrivé	I had arrived
j'étais venu	I had come
j'étais entré	I had entered
j'étais sorti	I had gone out
j'étais parti	I had left
j'étais monté	I had gone up
j'étais tombé	I had fallen

8. Help! Bring!

Aidez-moi!	Help me!
Apportez-moi encore du . . .	Bring me some more . . .
Apportez-le moi	Bring it to me.
Arrêtez!	Stop!
Arrêtez tout de suite!	Stop right away!
Arrêtez-vous là!	Stop there!
Arrêtez-le!	Stop him!
Asseyez-vous.	Sit down. Have a seat.
Croyez-moi.	Believe me.
Ecoutez!	Listen!
Ecoutez-moi.	Listen to me.
Ecoutez-moi bien.	Listen to me carefully.
Ecoutez-ça.	Listen to this (that).
Ecoutez-bien.	Listen carefully.
Ecoutez-le.	Listen to him.
Ne l'écoutez pas.	Don't listen (to him).
Ecoutez donc!	Listen! Listen, won't you.
Enlevez-ça!	Take that away!
Entrez!	Enter! Come in! Go in!
Envoyez-le lui!	Send it to him!

Envoyez-les moi!	Send them to me.
Envoyez-lui-en!	Send him some!
Envoyez-m'en!	Send me some!
Essayez!	Try!
N'essayez pas!	Don't try!
N'essayez pas de faire cela!	Don't try to do that!
Lavez-vous!	Wash yourself!
Levez-vous!	Stand up! Get up!
Lisez-ça!	Read that!
Menez-y moi	Take me there!
Montez-y!	Go up there!
Montrez-moi!	Show me!
Montrez-moi ça!	Show me it (that)!
Montrez-le moi!	Show it to me!
Montrez-lui.	Show him.
Ne le lui montrez pas!	Don't show it to him!
N'oubliez pas!	Don't forget!
Partez!	Leave!
Partez vite!	Leave quickly! Go right away!
Ne partez pas!	Don't leave! Don't go!
Passez!	Pass! Go in!
Pensez-y!	Think about it!
Permettez-moi de vous présenter . . .	Allow me to present . . .
Vous permettez?—Faites!	May I?—Of course!
Portez-ça là-bas.	Carry this over there.
Prenez!	Take!
Prenez-le!	Take it!
Ne le prenez pas.	Don't take it.

Prenez-en encore un.	Take another one.
Prenez le train.	Take the train.
Prenez un taxi.	Take a taxi.
Ne prenez pas la peine.	Don't trouble yourself. ("Don't take the trouble.")
Regardez!	Look!
Regardez encore!	Look again!
Regardez ici!	Look here!
Regardez-moi!	Look at me!
Regardez-ça.	Look at this (that).
Ne regardez pas.	Don't look.
Rendez-le moi.	Return it to me.
Rentrez chez vous!	Go home!
Rentrez tôt!	Go home early!
Répétez!	Repeat! Say it again!
Répétez-ça.	Repeat it (this, that). Say it (this, that) again.
Restez!	Stay!
Restez ici.	Stay here.
Restez tranquille.	Be still.
Sortez!	Go out!
Suivez!	Follow!
Suivez-moi.	Follow me.
Suivez-le.	Follow him.
Ne touchez pas!	Don't touch!
Versez-moi du café.	Pour me some coffee.

The *-ez* form corresponds to *vous —ez,* that is, it is the formal form. The familiar form, the one that corresponds to the *tu* form, is as follows:

Donner to give

tu donnes	you give
Donne!	Give!

Finir to finish

tu finis	you finish
Finis!	Finish!

Prendre to take

tu prends	you take
Prends!	Take!

9. Giving, Speaking, Being

donnant	giving
parlant	speaking
étant	being
ayant	having
faisant	doing
disant	saying
voyant	seeing
venant	coming

Eau courante.	Running water.
Suivant l'usage . . .	Following the custom . . .
Revenant au sujet principal . . .	Coming back to the main subject . . .
Quelqu'un habitant Paris.	Someone living in Paris.
Je termine en espérant recevoir bientôt de vos nouvelles.	I close hoping to hear from you soon.

Notice that the *-ant* form corresponds to our "*-ing*" form in English.

10. Let's

Allons-y!	Let's go there!
Allons là-bas!	Let's go over there!
Voyons!	Let's see!
Partons!	Let's leave!
Essayons!	Let's try!
Attendons!	Let's wait!
Prenons-en!	Let's take some!

QUIZ 32

1. *Montrez-moi*	1. Look at this (that).
2. *Passez!*	3. Look here.
3. *Vous permettez?—Faites donc!*	3. Take a taxi.
4. *Pensez-y.*	4. Take another one.
5. *Permettez-moi de vous présenter . . .*	5. Take it.
6. *Prenez-le.*	6. Allow me to present . . .
7. *Prenez un taxi.*	7. May I?—Go ahead! (Please do!)
8. *Prenez-en encore un.*	8. Think about it.
9. *Regardez ici.*	9. Pass! Go in!
10. *Regardez-ça.*	10. Show me.

ANSWERS

1—10; 2—9; 3—7; 4—8; 5—6; 6—5; 7—3; 8—4; 9—2; 10—1.

85. MEETING AN OLD FRIEND

(Meeting an Old Friend)

Rencontre de deux camarades
Meeting of two friends

1. **G: Tiens, vous voilà. . . . Comment ça va, mon cher ami?**
   G: Oh, there you are! How are you?

2. **L: Et vous, mon vieux?**
   L: How are you?

3. **G: Pas trop fatigante cette traversée?**
   G: Not too tired from your trip?

4. **L: Ma foi non!**
   L: Not at all.

5. **G: Je vais vous présenter à ma femme.**
   G: I'd like you to meet my wife.

6. **L: Avec plaisir.**
   L: I'd be very happy to.

7. **G: Chérie, je te présente Jean Lenoir.**
   G: This is Jean Lenoir, dear.

8. **L: Très heureux de faire votre connaissance, Madame.**
   L: I'm very happy to know you.

9. **Mme G: Et moi aussi, Monsieur.**
   Mrs. G: Glad to know you.

10. **L: J'ai beaucoup de plaisir à vous revoir, vous savez.**
    L: It's really very good to see you again.

11. **G: Et moi donc. Vous n'avez pas changé.**
    G: I'm certainly glad to see you. You haven't

changed a bit.

12. **L: Et vous non plus.**
L: Neither have you.

13. **Mme G: Madame Lenoir se plaît-elle aux Etats-Unis?**
Mrs. G: How does Mrs. Lenoir like the United States?

14. **L: Beaucoup.**
L: She likes it a lot.

15. **Mme G: Ça ne ressemble guère à Paris?**
Mrs. G: It must be very different from Paris.

16. **L: Certainement il y a de drôles de choses aux Etats-Unis.**
L: There certainly are lots of very curious things in the United States!

17. **Mme G: Par exemple?**
Mrs. G: For example?

18. **L: Par exemple, vous n'auriez certainement pas l'idée d'aller déjeuner dans une pharmacie?**
L: For example, it certainly wouldn't occur to you to have lunch in a pharmacy.

19. **G: Vous blaguez!**
G: You're joking!

20. **L: Pas du tout, je suis très sérieux.**
L: Not at all. I'm very serious.

21. **Mme G: Quoi? Racontez-nous ça. Vous dites . . . déjeuner . . . dans une pharmacie?**
Mrs. G: Come, tell us about it! You say . . . one has lunch . . . in a pharmacy?

22. **L: Oui, chère Madame, même avec un bif-tec. . . .**

L: Yes, you can even have a steak. . . .

23. **G: Dans une pharmacie?**
G: In a pharmacy?

24. **L: Oui, oui, dans une pharmacie, et pour dessert vous pouvez avoir une excellent glace. . . .**
L: Yes, in a pharmacy—with excellent ice cream for dessert.

25. **Mme G: Mais l'odeur de la pharmacie? . . . ça ne vous gêne pas . . . ?**
Mrs. G: But the smell of the pharmacy—doesn't that bother you?

26. **L: Il n'y a pas d'odeur dans nos. . . .**
L: There isn't any smell in our . . .

27. **G: Pharmacies?**
G: . . . pharmacies?

28. **L: D'ailleurs nous ne les appelons pas pharmacies mais "drug stores."**
L: No. ("Moreover") we don't call them pharmacies but "drug stores."

29. **G: Ah, nous y voilà! Ils leur donnent un autre nom!**
G: Oh! That's the trick! They give them a different name!

30. **Mme G: Mais qu'est-ce que ça y change?**
Mrs. G: But how does that change things?

31. **G: Eh bien, il n'y a plus de pharmacie!**
G: Then it's no longer a pharmacy!

32. **L: Dans un "drug store" vous trouverez également un tas de choses: des jouets, des timbres-poste, des cigarettes. . . .**

L: You also find many other things in a drug store: toys, stamps, cigarettes. . . .

33. G: Que c'est drôle!
G: That's really very funny.

34. L: Des livres, de la papeterie, des ustensiles de cuisine, des articles de toilette, que sais-je encore . . . ?
L: Books, stationery, cooking utensils, toilet articles and what-have-you.

35. G: C'est un bazar alors?
G: It's a bazaar, then?

36. L: Mais non, mon cher, c'est un "drug store!"
L: No, it's (still) a drug store!

NOTES

Title: *Recontre de deux vieux camarades.* "Meeting of two old friends."

1. *Mon cher* (fem. *Ma chère)* my dear. The addition of *mon* or *ma* before *cher* makes the expression more friendly; *cher ami* is more formal than *Mon cher ami. Mon cher* is used only with people you know very well.
2. *Vieux* old; old fellow. *Mon vieux* is used only to someone you know extremely well.—In English greetings usually run as follows: "How are you?"—"Fine, thanks. How are you?"—"Very well, thanks." In French, however, one person says "How are you?" the other says "And you?" and then the conversation continues.
3. "Not too tiring, your trip?"—that is, "Your trip wasn't too tiring, I hope." In French *cette* ("this") is often used where in English we say "the" or, as in this case, "your." *Traversée* crossing.

4. *Ma foi non.* "My faith, no."
5. *Je vais vous présenter à . . .* "I am going to introduce you to . . ." The common formula is: *Permettez-moi de vous présenter Monsieur X.* Allow me to introduce Mr. X to you. I'd like you to meet Mr. X.
6. *Avec plaisir.* "With pleasure." *Avec grand plaisir.* "With great pleasure." = *Je serais en effet très heureux.* "I would really be very happy." = *Je serais très honoré.* "I would be greatly honored."
7. *Chérie* (fem.) my darling.
8. *Très heureux de faire votre connaissance.* "Very happy to make your acquaintance." = *Très heureux de vous connaître.* "Very happy to know you."
9. *Et moi aussi.* "And I too."
10. *J'ai beaucoup de plaisir.* "I have much pleasure." *Vous savez.* "You know." Notice this use of the expression.
12. *Plus* more. *Vous non plus.* Neither (have) you.
13. *Madame Lenoir se plaît-elle . . . ?* Does Mrs. Lenoir like . . . ?
15. "It hardly resembles Paris." *Ne . . . guère.* Hardly. Scarcely.
18. *Vous auriez* you would have; from *avoir* to have. *Vous n'auriez pas l'idée.* ("You wouldn't have the idea.") It wouldn't occur to you.
21. *Déjeuner* to have lunch.
25. *L'odeur de pharmacie* "The smell of a pharmacy." *Gêner* to bother. *Ça ne vous gêne pas?* Doesn't that bother you? *Mes souliers me gênent.* My shoes bother me. Other meanings: *Etre gêné* to be embarrassed. *Ne vous gênez pas.* Don't feel embarrassed!

Go right ahead! Make yourself at home! Make yourself comfortable! In the last meaning = *Faites comme chez vous.* Make yourself at home.

28. *D'ailleurs* besides; moreover.

29. *Nous y voilà!* ("There we are!") That's it! That's the trick.

30. "But how does that change things?"

32. *Trouverez* you will find. *Egalement* equally; also.—*Un tas* a heap, a pile. Notice the use of *des: des jouets* toys, *des timbres* postage stamps, etc. (see page 44).

33. *Que c'est drôle!* How strange! How funny!

34. *Que sais-je encore?* "What else do I know?" *Sais-je* do I know; from *savoir* to know (see page 248).

35. *Alors* then.

QUIZ 33

1. *Tiens, vous* —— (there you are).
a. donc
b. voici
c. voilà

2. —— (how) *ça va, mon cher ami?*
a. voilá
b. comment
c. vous

3. *Pas trop* —— (tiring), *cette traversée?*
a. monde
b. connaissance
c. fatigante

4. *Je vais vous presenter à ma* —— (wife).
   a. *femme*
   b. *moins*
   c. *joie*

5. *J'ai beaucoup de* —— (pleasure) *de vous revoir.*
   a. *change*
   b. *plaisir*
   c. *même*

6. *Il y a des* —— (things) *bien curieuses.*
   a. *bien*
   b. *doit*
   c. *choses*

7. *Je suis* —— (very) *sérieux.*
   a. *très*
   b. *mais*
   c. *tout*

8. *Nous ne les* —— (call) *pas pharmacies.*
   a. *appelons*
   b. *ailleurs*
   c. *change*

9. *C'est un bazar* —— (then).
   a. *alors*
   b. *mais*
   c. *encore*

10. *Trés heureux de faire votre* —— (acquaintance).
    a. *d'ailleurs*
    b. *connaissance*
    c. *monde*

ANSWERS

1—c; 2—b; 3—c; 4—a; 5—b; 6—c; 7—a; 8—a; 9—a; 10—b.

86. THE COMMONEST VERBS

1. *Voir* to see

je vois	*nous voyons*
tu vois	*vous voyez*
il voit	*ils voient*

Voyons.
Let's see.

Je ne vois pas.
I don't see.

Il voit tout.
He sees everything.

L'avez-vous jamais vu?
Have you ever seen him (her)?

Je viens de la voir.
I've just seen her.

Je ne vois pas ce que vous voulez dire.
I don't see what you mean.

Je vois ce que vous voulez dire.
I see what you mean.

Qui est-ce que vous voyez?
Qui voyez-vous?
Whom do you see?

Pouvez-vous me voir maintenant?
Can you see me now?

Venez nous voir un soir.
Come to see us some evening.

2. *Savoir* to know

je sais	*nous savons*
tu sais	*vous savez*
il sait	*ils savent*

Je le sais.
I know it.

Je ne sais pas.
I don't know.

Je le sais bien.
I know it very well.

Il ne sait rien.
He doesn't know anything.

Je n'en sais rien.
I don't know anything about it.

Je sais qu'il est ici.
I know that he's here.

Savez-vous ça?
Do you know that?

Savez-voux où il est?
Do you know where he is?

Qui sait?
Who knows?

Il n'en sait pas davantage
He doesn't know any more about it.

Il n'en sait pas plus que vous.
He doesn't know any more about it than you do.

3. *Tenir* to hold

je tiens	*nous tenons*
tu tiens	*vous tenez*
il tient	*ils tiennent*

Tenez-moi ça un instant.
Hold this for me a minute.

Il tient son chapeau à la main.
He's holding his hat in his hand.

Je le tiens maintenant.
I have it now.

Tenez bon!
Hold firm!

Il faut tenir
We must hold on.

Ne quittez pas!
Hold the wire a minute.

Tenez-vous tranquille!
Keep quiet! Keep still!

Tenez!—Pas plus tard qu'hier . . .
Look, only yesterday . . . ("Not later than yesterday . . .")

Tenez, voilà votre argent.
Look, here's your money.

Tiens! Voilà pour toi.
Look, here's something for you.

Tiens, le voilà.
Look, there he is.

Il tient à elle.
He likes her.

Il tient à le faire.
He's anxious to do it. He's set on doing it.

Il se le tient pour dit.
He takes it for granted.

Tenez cela pour fait.
Consider it done.

Je le tiens de bonne source.
I have it from a good source. I have it on good authority.

Tenez votre droite.
Keep to your right.

Tiens ta promesse.
Keep your *(fam.)* promise.

4. *Pouvoir* to be able

je peux or *puis*	*nous pouvons*
tu peux	*vous pouvez*
il peut	*ils peuvent*

Je ne peux pas.
I can't.

Je peux le faire.
I can do it.

Pouvez-vous me dire si . . .
Can you tell me if . . .

Pouvez-vous venir?
Can you come?

Je ne vois pas comment il peut faire cela.
I don't see how he can do that.

Je ne peux pas répondre à la question.
I can't answer the question.

Vous pouvez le faire sans difficulté.
You can do it without any difficulty.

Je ne peux pas y aller.
I can't go there.

Quand pouvons-nous partir?
When can we leave?

Vous pouvez y aller.
You can go there.

Pouvez-vous m'aider?
Can you help me?

5. *Comprendre* to understand

je comprends	*nous comprenons*
tu comprends	*vous comprenez*
il comprend	*ils comprennent*

Il ne comprend pas.
He doesn't understand.

Je comprends très bien.
I understand very well.

Je ne vous comprends pas.
I don't understand you.

Vous ne me comprenez pas?
Don't you understand me?

Comprenez-vous?
Do you understand?

Comprenez-vous le français?
Do you understand Franch?

Comprenez-vous l'anglais?
Do you understand English?

Comprenez-vous tout ce qu'il vous dit?
Do you understand everything he's saying to you?

Je n'ai pas compris.
I don't understand. ("I haven't understood. I didn't understand.")

Avez-vous compris?
Did you understand? ("Have you understood?" "Did you understand?")

Je ne peux pas me faire comprendre.
I can't make myself understood.

Il ne comprend rien aux affaires.
He doesn't understand anything about business.

Compris?
Did you understand? Do you understand?

Je n'y comprends rien.
I don't understand it at all. I don't understand anything about it. It's a mystery to me. I'm all in the dark.

6. *Mettre* to put or place

Je mets	*nous mettons*
tu mets	*vous mettez*
il met	*ils mettent*

Mettez-le là.
Put it there.

Où l'avez-vous mis?
Where did you put it?

Mettez votre chapeau.
Put your hat on.

Mettez-le.
Put it on.

Elle a mis la table.
She set the table.

Il a mis son nouveau costume.
He put on his new suit.

Il ne sait jamais où il met ses affaires.
He never knows where he puts (his) things.

Mettons-nous à table.
Let's sit down to eat. ("Let's sit down to the table.")

7. *Connaître* to know

je connais	*nous connaissons*
tu connais	*vous connaissez*
il connaît	*ils connaissent*

Je le connais.
I know it.

Je ne le connais pas.
I don't know it.

Je ne connais personne dans cette ville.
I don't know anyone in this city.

Je connais sa famille.
I know this family.

Tout le monde le connaît.
Everybody knows it.

Je le connais de vue.
I know him by sight.

Je le connais de nom.
I know him by name.

C'est très connu.
It's very well known.

Ce n'est pas bien connu en France.
That's not very well known in France.

C'est inconnu.
It's unknown.

8. *Vouloir* to want

je veux	*nous voulons*
tu veux	*vous voulez*
il vent	*ils veulent*

Je le veux.
I want it. I insist on it.

Je ne le veux pas.
I don't want it.

Je ne veux rien.
I don't want anything.

J'en veux.
I want some.

Il n'en veut pas.
He doesn't want any of it.

Il le peut mais il ne le veut pas.
He can do it but he doesn't want to.

Voulez-vous?
Do you want to?

Que voulez-vous?
What do you want (wish)? What would you like?

Il veut revenir?
Does he want to return?

Voulez-vous venir avec nous?
Do you want to come with us?

Voulez-vous venir déjeuner avec nous?
Will you have lunch with us?

Voulez-vous venir samedi?
Will you come Saturday?

Qui est-ce qui veut cela (ça)?
Who wants that?

Qu'est-ce que vous voulez dire?
What do you mean? ("What do you want to say?")

Voulez-vous me suivre?
Will you please follow me?

Comme vous voulez.
As you wish.

C'est comme vous voulez.
As you wish. Whatever you say.

Si vous voulez.
If you wish. If you want to.

9. *Devoir* to owe or to have to

je dois	*nous devons*
tu dois	*vous devez*
il doit	*ils doivent*

Je dois partir maintenant.
I have to go now.

Il doit venir.
He should (has to) come.

Il devrait être ici.
He should (has to) be here.

Ils doivent être là.
They have to (should, ought to) be there.

Devez-vous y aller?
Do you have to go (there)?

Qu'est-ce que je dois faire?
What do I have to do?

Combien est-ce que je vous dois?
Combien vous dois-je?
How much do I owe you?

Vous me devez cent francs.
You owe me 100 francs.

Il me doit dix francs.
He owes me 10 francs.

Vous ne me devez rien.
You don't owe me anything.

10. *Attendre* to wait

Attendez ici.
Wait here.

Attendez là.
Wait there.

Attendez-le.
Wait for it (him).

Attendez-moi.
Wait for me.

Attendez un peu.
Wait a little.

Attendez un moment.
Wait a minute.

N'attendez pas.
Don't wait.

Je l'attends.
I'm waiting for him.

Elle attend les autres.
She's waiting for the others.

Qui attendez-vous?
Whom are you waiting for?

Pourquoi est-ce que vous attendez?
Why are you waiting?

Je m'excuse de vous avoir fait attendre.
I'm sorry I kept you waiting. ("I apologize for making you wait.")

11. *Demander* to ask

Demandez là-bas.
Ask over there.

Demandez-le là-bas.
Ask about (for) it (him) over there.

Qu'est-ce qu'il demande?
What's he asking? What's he want?

Il ne demande rien.
He's not asking for anything. He doesn't want anything.

Demandez votre chemin si vous vous perdez.
Ask your way if you get lost.

Demandez-lui de vous faire de la monnaie.
Ask him to give you change.

Demandez-lui l'heure.
Ask him the time.

Demandez-lui du feu.
Ask him for a light.

Allez-le lui demander.
Go and ask him ("it").

Si on me demande, je reviens dans un instant.
If someone asks for me, I'll be back in a moment.

Il a demandé où c'est.
He asked where it is.

Combien coûte ce livre?
How much is this book?

Il en demande cent francs.
He's asking a hundred francs for it.

Demandez-le au téléphone.
Call him on the phone.

On vous demande.
Someone is asking for you. You're wanted.

On vous demande au téléphone.
You're wanted on the telephone.

Je vous demande pardon.
I beg your pardon.

Je me demande si c'est vrai.
I wonder if it's true. ("I ask myself if . . .")

Je me demande pourquoi il ne vient pas.
I wonder why he doesn't come.

C'est ce que je me demande.
That's what I'd like to know.

Je vous demande un peu!
I ask you! How do you like that!

Je ne demande pas mieux.
I ask nothing better. I'm willing. I'll do it gladly. I'd be delighted. It's all right with me. ("I don't ask better.")

12. *Aimer* to love or to like

Il l'aime.
He loves her. He's in love with her.

Est-ce que vous l'aimez?
Do you like him (her, it)?

Je n'aime pas cela.
I don't like it (that).

J'aime mieux l'autre.
I like the other better.

J'aime mieux y aller ce soir.
I'd rather go there this evening. I'd prefer to go there this evening.

13. *Falloir* to be necessary.

Il faut.
It's necessary. You must. You have to. One must. One has to.

Faut-il y aller?
Is it necessary to go? Do I (you, we, etc.) have to go?

Faut-il venir?
Should I (you, we, etc.) come?

Il faut venir.
You (I, we, etc.) have to come.

Combien de temps faut-il pour aller de Paris à Londres?
How long does it take to go from Paris to London?

Qu'est-ce qu'il faut faire?
What's to be done? What am I to do?

Comme il faut.
As is proper. As it should be.

Un homme comme il faut.
A respectable man.

Des gens comme il faut.
Well-bred people ("people as they should be").

Faites cela comme il faut.
Do it properly. Do it the way it should be done.

14. *Valoir* to be worth

Ça vaut combien?
How much is it worth?

Qu'est-ce que ça vaut?
What's that worth?

Ça vaut cent francs.
It's worth a hundred francs.

Ça ne vaut pas un sou.
It's not worth a cent.

Ça ne vaut pas un clou.
It's not worth a hang ("a nail").

Ça ne vaut rien.
It's (that's) not worth anything. That's no good.

Ça ne vaut pas grand'chose.
It's no good.

Ça ne vaut rien.
It's not worth anything. It's worthless.

Ça vaut son prix.
It's not worth the money. ("It's worth its price.")

Ça vaut très cher.
It's worth a lot of money.

Ça ne vaut pas ça.
It's not worth that.

Ça ne vaut pas la peine.
It isn't worth while. It isn't worth the trouble.

87. COMMON NOTICES AND SIGNS

Avis au public	Public Notice
Messieurs / *Hommes*	Men
Dames	Women
Toilettes pour hommes	Men's Room
Toilettes pour dames	Ladies' Room
W. C.	Toilet
Fumeurs	Smokers
Non fumeurs	Non-Smokers
Défense de fumer	No Smoking
Ouvert	Open
Fermé	Closed
Clôture	Closing
Entrée	Entrance
Sortie	Exit
Sortie de secours	Emergency Exit
Ascenseur	Elevator
Rez-de-chaussée	Ground Floor
Tirez	Pull
Poussez	Push
Tournez	Turn
Sonnez S.V.P.	Please Ring
Défense d'entrer	Keep Out
Entrez	Come In
Entrez sans frapper	Come In Without Knocking
Sonnez et tournez le bouton	Ring and Turn the Knob
Frappez	Knock
Frappez avant d'entrer	Knock Before Entering
Sonnez avant d'entrer	Ring Before Entering
Prière de . . .	You Are Requested To . . .

Fermé pour cause de réparations	Closed For Repair
Changement de propriétaire	Under New Management
Interdit au public / *Entrée interdite*	No Admittance
Ouverture prochaine / *Sera ouvert prochainement*	Will be Opened Shortly
Ouvert toute la nuit	Open All Night
Défense de cracher	No Spitting
Essuyez-vous les pieds	Wipe Your Feet
Tenez les chiens en laisse	Keep Your Dog on Leash
Interdit aux piétons	Pedestrians Keep Out
Défense de pénétrer dans la proprieté	No Trespassing
Bureau de réclamations / *Réclamations*	Complaint Department
Adressez-vous au guichet / *S'adresser au guichet*	Apply at the Window
Bureau de change	Money Exchanged
A vendre	For Sale
A louer présentement	For Rent. For Immediate Rental
Appartement à louer	Unfurnished Apartment to Let
Appartement meublé à louer	Furnished Apartment to Let
Soldes	Bargains
Rabais	Reductions
En vente ici	On Sale Here
Vestiaire	Check Room *(in a hotel, restaurant or café)*

Billard	Billiard Room
Concierge	Janitor
Consigne	Cloakroom
Circulation détournée	Detour
Route en réparation *Route en rechargement*	Road in Repair
Tournant dangereux	Dangerous Curve
Défense de stationner	No parking
Sens unique	One-Way Street
Défense de traverser les voies	Do Not Cross the Tracks
Passage à niveau	Railroad Crossing, Grade Crossing
Voie ferrée	Railroad
Passage souterrain	Underpass
Halte	Stop
Attention	Caution
Passage clouté	Pedestrian Crossing
Carrefour	Crossroads
Défense d'afficher	Post No Bills
Vitesse maximum 20 km	Maximum Speed 20 Kilometers Per Hour
Allure modérée	Go Slow
Attention écoles	School—Go Slow
Danger	Danger
Sens interdit	No Thoroughfare
Prenez garde à la peinture	Fresh Paint
Arrêt facultatif	Stop on Signal
Arrêt obligatoire	Stop Here
Ne pas se pencher au dehors	Don't Lean Out of the Window
Signal d'alarme	Alarm Signal

Haute tension	High Voltage
Métro / *Métropolitain*	Subway
Consigne	Baggage Room. Check Room *(in a railroad station).*
Salle d'attente	Waiting Room
1ère classe[1]	First Class
2e classe	Second Class
Arrivée	Arrival
Départ	Departure
Quai	Platform
Bureau de renseignements	Information
Bureau de location	Ticket Office
Bureau de postes	Post Office
Boîte aux lettres	Mail Box
Contrôle	Box Office
Avertisseur d'incendie	Fire Box
Bibliothèque municipale	Public Library
Poste, télégraphe, téléphone (P.T.T.)	Post Office, Telegraph, Telephone
Commissariat de police	Police Station
Essence	Gas Station
Librairie	Bookstore
Mairie	City Hall
Coiffeur	Barber Shop. Hair Dresser
Docteur-médecin	Physician
Chirurgien-dentiste	Dentist
Cordonnerie	Shoe Repairing

[1] Different kinds of railway coaches.

Aujourd'hui matinée	Matinee Today
Matinée à 2h30	Matinee at 2:30
Soirée à 8h30	Evenings at 8:30
Tenue de soirée obligatoire / *Tenue de soirée de rigueur*	Formal Dress
Tenue de ville	Informal Dress
Spectacle permanent	Continuous Performance
Relâche	Closed (used for theatres only). No Performance
Changement de programme	Change of Program
Apéritifs	Cocktails (Served Here)
Table d'hôte	Table d'hôte
Vin compris	Wine included in the price
Buffet	Refreshments

FINAL QUIZ

1. ———(how) *allez-vous?*

a. comme
b. comment
c. quànd

2. ——— (speak) *lentement.*

a. parlez
b. parler
c. parles

3. ——— (have) *-vous des cigarettes?*
   a. *j'ai*
   b. *avoir*
   c. *avez*

4. *Donnez-* ——— (me) *la carte.*
   a. *moi*
   b. *me*
   c. *le*

5. ——— (I'd like) *une tasse de café.*
   a. *je veux*
   b. *je voudrais*
   c. *je vais*

6. *Nous voudrions* ——— (breakfast) *pour trois personnes.*
   a. *le déjeuner*
   b. *le petit déjeuner*
   c. *le dîner*

7. ——— (bring) *-moi une cuillère à café.*
   a. *donnez*
   b. *apportez*
   c. *pouvez*

8. *Où se trouve* ——— (the station)?
   a. *la route*
   b. *la gare*
   c. *le bureau*

9. ——— (are you) *certain?*
   a. *faites-vous*
   b. *dites-vous*
   c. *êtes-vous*

10. ——— (I have) *assez de temps.*
a. je suis
b. j'ai
c. je vais

11. ——— (does he have) *de l'argent?*
a. il y a
b. est-il
c. a-t-il

12. ——— (are there) *des lettres pour moi?*
a. il y a
b. y a-t-il
c. a-t-il

13. Est-ce que vous ——— (understand)?
a. comprends
b. comprenez
c. étendez

14. Je suis——— (happy) *de faire votre connaissance.*
a. heureux
b. enchanté
c. honoré

15. En voulez-vous peu ou ——— (a lot)?
a. encore
b. beaucoup
c. assez

16. Qu'est-ce que vous ——— (say)?
a. faites
b. dites
c. dire

17. *Comment* —— (does one say) *cela en français?*
    a. *dites-vous*
    b. *dit-on*
    c. *écrit-on*

18. *Leur numéro de téléphone est Littré* —— (3307)
    a. *vingt-six, seize*
    b. *trente-trois, zéro sept*
    c. *trente-six, quarante-deux*

19. —— (I need) *de cela.*
    a. *j'ai envie*
    b. *j'en ai*
    c. *j'ai besoin*

20. *Je reviendrai* —— (tomorrow morning).
    a. *aprés-midi*
    b. *demain matin*
    c. *hier soir*

21. —— (it's necessary) *voir le gérant pour cela.*
    a. *il y a*
    b. *il faut*
    c. *y a-t-il*

22. *Je vous* —— (ask) *pardon.*
    a. *demande*
    b. *prie*
    c. *dit*

23. *Comment vous* —— (call)-*vous.*
    a. *appelez*
    b. *demandez*
    c. *écrivez*

24. ——— (the check) *s'il vous plaît.*
   a. *le beurre*
   b. *l'argent*
   c. *l'addition*

25. *Voulez-vous me* ——— (give) *une serviette?*
   a. *apporter*
   b. *donner*
   c. *passer*

ANSWERS

1—b; 2—a; 3—c; 4—a; 5—b; 6—b; 7—b; 8—b; 9—c; 10—b; 11—c; 12—b; 13—b; 14—a; 15—b; 16—b; 17—b; 18—b; 19—c; 20—b; 21—b; 22—a; 23—a; 24—c; 25—b.

WHEN YOU GET 100% ON THIS QUIZ YOU CAN CONSIDER THAT YOU HAVE MASTERED THE COURSE.

SUMMARY OF FRENCH GRAMMAR

About the Sounds

Very few sounds are exactly alike in both English and French. The pronunciation equivalents given below can therefore be only approximate. Although exceptions exist for almost every pronunciation rule, the guidelines in this section should prove useful to the student.

The Consonants. French consonant sounds are generally softer than those of English. A number of them are produced by bringing the tongue in contact with different parts of the mouth cavity than for the equivalent English consonant, or by changing the pressure of the airstream. For example, the English speaker produces the sound of *d, t,* or *n* by placing the tip of the tongue *against the gum ridge behind* the upper teeth. The French speaker produces these sounds by placing the tip of the tongue *against the back* of the upper teeth.

In pronouncing a *p* at the beginning of a word such as "pat" or "pen," the English speaker produces a puff of air, whereas the French speaker does not. Try holding your hand in front of your mouth and say the words "pit," "pack," and "punch." You will feel the puff of air each time you say the *p* at the beginning of each of these words. The French speaker, on the other hand, produces the *p* at the beginning of words *without* the puff of air. The French *p* is close in sound to the English *p* in words like "speak" or "spot."

The pronunciation of the sound *l* also varies in the two languages. American English has two *l* sounds—one which is used at the beginning of a word (the "light" *l*), and another which is used in the middle or at the end of a word (the "dark" *l*). Contrast the *l* sound in the words "like" and "beautiful." The *l* in "like" is a "light" *l*, and this is the *l* sound pronounced in French.

The Vowels. Some of the vowel sounds of French resemble the vowels in English. Many vowel sounds, however, are quite different, and some do not exist in English at all. For example, the sound represented by *é* resembles the English *ay* in the word "day," but the two sounds are not the same. When an English speaker says "day," he is actually pronouncing two sounds: an *a* and a *y*, which glide together to form a diphthong. Try holding your hand on your jaw and saying the words listed below. As you do so, notice how your jaw closes up a bit toward the end of the *ay* sound:

day say may ray nay tray jay

In French, however, the jaw does not move as you say the *é* sound; it remains steady. Pronounce the following French words, while holding the jaw still.

des bébé fâché mes réalité

A similar phenomenon occurs with the sound *o*. Say the following words in English:

bow tow know so

Note that the jaw rises at the end of the sound as though to close on the sound *w*. Hold your hand on your jaw and say the above words "in slow motion." Now, leaving off the *w* sound at the end by holding the jaw steady, say the following words in French:

beau tôt nos sot (the final consonants are silent)

Space does not permit us to compare every English sound with its French counterpart, but the charts below will help to clarify the sounds. Repeated imitation of the speakers on the recordings will be most important in your learning to pronounce French correctly.

1. THE ALPHABET

Letter	Name	Letter	Name	Letter	Name
a	a	**j**	ji	**s**	esse
b	be	**k**	ka	**t**	te
c	ce	**l**	elle	**u**	u
d	de	**m**	emme	**v**	ve
e	e	**n**	enne	**w**	double ve
f	effe	**o**	o	**x**	iks
g	ge	**p**	pe	**y**	i grec
h	ache	**q**	ku	**z**	zede
i	i	**r**	erre		

2. THE CONSONANTS

The letters *b, d, f, k, l, m, n, p, s, t, v,* and *z* are pronounced approximately as in English when they are not in final position, but with the differences indicated above. Note however:

c before *a, o, u, l,* and *r* is like the *c* in "cut." Ex., *carte, coeur, cuisine, clarté, croire*
before *e* and *i,* is like *s* in "see." Ex., *centre, cinéma*

ç (*c* with cedilla) is like *s* in "see." Ex., *français, garçon*

ch is like *sh* in "ship." Ex., *chéri, cheval*. But: *chr* is pronounced like English *kr*. Ex., *chrétien*

g before *a, o, u, l, r* is like *g* in "go." Ex., *gare, goût, guerre, glace, grand*
before *e* and *i*, is like the *s* sound in "measure." Ex., *genre, voyageur, Gigi*

gn is like *ni* in "onion" or *ny* in "canyon." Ex., *oignon, soigner*

h is not pronounced. Ex., *heure*

j is like the *s* sound in "measure." Ex., *bonjour, joie*

l is always "light" (as explained above) when it is pronounced as *l*. However, in the following combinations it is pronounced like the *y* in "yes": *-ail, -eil, -eille, -aille, -ille, -ill*. Ex., *chandail, vermeil, oreille, grisaille, vieillard*. But: in *mille, ville* the *l*'s are pronounced as *l*.

qu before *a, e, i, o, u* is like *k*. Ex., *qui, quotidien*
before *oi* is like *kwa*. Ex., *quoi*

r is made farther back in the throat than the English *r;* almost like a gargle. There is also the *trilled r*, which is used by some people in various parts of the country, particularly in the South. The *trilled r* is formed by the tip of the tongue against the gum ridge back of the upper teeth in a rapid succession of taps. Both ways of pronouncing *r* are considered correct.

s is generally like the *s* in "see." Ex., *soir, estimer*
between vowels is like the *s* in "rose." Ex., *rose, vase*

w (occurring only in foreign words) is generally pronounced *v*. Ex., *wagon*
is sometimes pronounced *w*. Ex., *whisky*

final consonants As a general rule, final consonants are silent. However, words ending in *c, f, l,* and *r* often do pronounce the final consonant. Ex.:
-c: parc, sac, trafic
-f: bref, chef, oeuf
-l: moral, Noël, journal
-r: sur, erreur, manoir
There are several cases in which the final *r* is generally silent:

1) The infinite ending of *-er* verbs. Ex., *parler, aller, jouer*
2) Names of certain tradespeople. Ex., *le boucher, le boulanger, le plombier*
3) Nouns ending in *-er*. Ex., *verger, soulier, tablier*

There are many common words ending in *c, l,* and *f* in which the final consonant is silent. Ex., *estomac, banc, blanc, gentil, pareil, clef*

3. SIMPLE VOWELS

a as in "ah!" or "father." Ex., *pâté, mâle, Jacques*
as in "marry." Ex., *ami, mal*

e as in "let." Ex., *belle, cher, cette*
as in "day," without the *y* sound at the end (as explained above). This occurs in monosyllables or words ending in *-er, -et,* or *-ez,* and is the same sound as *é*. Ex., *les, des, laver, filet, allez*
as in "the" (the "mute" *e* between two single consonants or in monosyllabic

words). Ex., *depuis, le, petit, tenir, besoin*

The unaccented *e* is silent ("mute") at the end of a word. Ex., *parle, femme, limonade*

é *(accent aigu)* as in "day," without the *y* sound at the end. Ex., *église, école, fâché, réalité*

è *(accent grave)* as in "let." Ex., *père, mètre, Agnès*

ê *(accent circonflexe)* as in "let." Ex., *tête, être*

i as in "machine." The letter *y*, when it acts as a vowel, is pronounced the same way. Ex., *machine, lycée, qui, bicyclette*

o (closed o) as in "go" (without the *w* sound at the end, as explained above). Ex., *tôt, mot, dos*

(open o) as in "north." Ex., *robe, alors, bonne, gosse*

u has no equivalent in English. To approximate the sound, say *ee,* keep the tongue in the position of *ee* (with the tip of the tongue against the bottom teeth), and then round the lips. Ex., *lune, nuit, assure*

ai as in "day" (without the *y* sound at the end). Ex., *mais, caisson, lait*

ei as in "let." Ex., *reine, peine*

au as in "go" (without the *w* sound at the end). Ex., *auprès, pauvre, eau, eau(x)*

eu has no equivalent in English. To approximate the sound, place the tongue as if for *é*, but round the lips as for *o*. Ex., *deux, feu, peu, ceux*

œ has no equivalent in English. It is more "open" than *eu*. To form the sound, place the tongue as if for the *e* of "let," but round the lips. This sound is usually followed by a consonant, as in *sœur, cœur*

oi pronounced *wa*. Ex., *moi, voilà*

ou as in "too." Ex., *nous, vous, cousin, rouge, amour*

4. THE NASALIZED VOWELS

When the consonants *n* and *m* are preceded by a vowel, the sound is generally nasalized; that is, the airstream escapes partly through the nose. The four categories of nasalized vowels are as follows:

1. *an, am, en* and *em* are like the vowel in *father* pronounced through the nose:

an	year
ample	ample
en	in
enveloppe	envelope
temps	time

2. *on* and *om* are like the vowel in *north* pronounced through the nose:

bon	good
tomber	to fall

3. *in, im, ein, eim, ain* and *aim* are like the vowel in *at* pronounced through the nose:

fin	end
simple	simple
faim	hunger
plein	full

4. *un* and *um* are like the vowel in *burn* pronounced through the nose:

un	one
chacun	each one
humble	humble

Vowels are nasalized in the following cases:

1. When the *n* or *m* is the final consonant or one of the final consonants:

fin	end
pont	bridge
champ	field
temps	time

2. In the middle of a word, when the *n* or *m* is not followed by a vowel:

NASALIZED

chambre	room	*impossible*	impossible

NOT NASALIZED

inutile	useless	*inoccupé*	unoccuied
initial	initial	*imitation*	imitation

Note: *mm* and *nn* do not cause the nasalization of the preceding vowel:

flamme	flame	*innocent*	innocent
donner	to give	*immense*	immense

Note: Most of the grammatical material outlined in the following pages is treated fully in the lessons.

5. THE APOSTROPHE

Certain one-syllable words ending in a vowel drop ("elide") the vowel when they come before words beginning with a vowel sound.

This dropping of the vowel or "elision" is marked by an apostrophe. Common cases are:

1. The *a* of *la:*

je l'aime	I like her (or it)	*l'heure*	the hour
l'amande	the almond		

2. The vowel *e* in one-syllable words *(le, je, se, me, que,* etc.*):*

l'argent	the money	*j'habite*	I live
j'ai	I have		

3. the vowel *i* in *si* "if," when it comes before *il* "he" or *ils* "they":

s'il vous plaît	please ("if it pleases you")

4. *moi* and *toi* when they come before *en* are written *m'* and *t':*

Donnez-m'en	Give me some of it (of them).

5. A few words like *aujourd'hui* today, *entr'acte* interlude, etc.

6. THE DEFINITE ARTICLE

	SINGULAR	PLURAL
Masculine	*le*	*les*
Feminine	*la*	*les*

SINGULAR

le garçon	the boy
la jeune fille	the young girl

PLURAL

les garçons	the boys
les jeunes filles	the young girls

1. *Le* and *la* become *l'* before words beginning with a vowel sound:

   This contraction takes place before most words beginning with *h* (this *h* is called "mute" *h*). There are a few words where this contraction does not occur (this *h* is called "aspirate" *h*):

l'ami	the friend	*l'heure*	the hour
le héros	the hero	*la hache*	the axe

2. Unlike English, the definite article is used in French before a noun used in a general

sense, before titles, days of the week, parts of the body, etc.:

l'avocat	the lawyer
l'avion	the airplane
le dimanche	Sunday (*or* Sundays)
le Comte . . .	Count . . .
J'aime les livres	I like books
Le fer est utile.	Iron is useful.
L'avarice est un vice.	Avarice is a vice.
Je vais me laver les mains.	I'm going to wash my hands.

3. The definite article is used with names of languages, unless preceded by *en:*

Le français est difficile.	French is difficult.

But—

Elle ranconte l'histoire en français.	She tells the story in French.

Note: The article is usually omitted with the name of a language used immediately after the verb *parler:*

Elle parle français.	She speaks French.

4. Unlike English, the definite articles must be repeated before each noun they modify.

les portes et les fenêtres	the doors and windows

7. THE INDEFINITE ARTICLE

	SINGULAR	PLURAL
Masculine	*un*	*des*
Feminine	*une*	*des*

SINGULAR

un homme	a man
une femme	a woman

PLURAL

des hommes	men; some men; a few men
des femmes	women; some women; a few women

1. The indefinite article is omitted before an unmodified statement of profession, nationality, rank, etc.:

Je suis médicin.	I am a doctor.
Elle est américaine.	She is an American.
Il est capitaine.	He is a captain.

2. The indefinite articles are repeated before each noun:

un homme et une femme	a man and woman

8. THE POSSESSIVE

The possessive is expressed in the following way: state the thing possessed + *de* ("of") + the possessor:

le livre de Marie	Mary's book ("the book of Mary")
la plume de l'élève	the pupil's pen ("the pen of the pupil")

9. CONTRACTIONS

1. The preposition *de* "of" combines with the definite articles *le* and *les* as follows:

de + le = du:	*le livre du professeur*	the teacher's book
de + les = des:	*les plumes des élèves*	the pupil's pens

2. The preposition *a* "to" combines with the articles *le* and *les* as follows:

a + le = au:	*Il parle au garçon.*	He's talking to the boy.
a + les = aux:	*Il parle aux garçons.*	He's talking to the boys.

10. GENDER

All English nouns take the articles *the* or *a(n)*. Adjectives modifying English nouns do not change their form. In French, however, all nouns show gender *(masculine or feminine),* and adjectives agree with nouns in gender and number *(singular or plural).*

Masculine nouns: Take the definite article *le* in the singular and *les* in the plural, and the indefinite artcile *un*. They are modified by the masculine form of an adjective.

Ex., *le costume brun*	the brown suit
les costumes bruns	the brown suits

Feminine nouns: Take the definite article *la* in the singular and *les* in the plural, and the indefinite article *une*. They are modified by the feminine form of an adjective.

Ex., *la robe brune*	the brown dress
les robes brunes	the brown dresses

<u>The gender of each noun must be learned with the noun.</u> The following tables describing which noun classes are masculine and which are feminine provide a general rule of thumb. There are a number of exceptions to each statement.

The following classes of nouns are generally masculine.

1. Nouns naming a male person. Ex., *le père* father, *le roi* king.
   But: *la sentinelle* sentinel
2. Nouns ending in a consonant. Ex., *le parc* park, *le pont* bridge, *le tarif* rate, tariff
   But: Nouns ending in *-ion* and *-son* are generally feminine. Ex., *l'action* action, *la conversation* conversation, *la raison* reason
3. Nouns ending in any vowel except "mute" *e*. Ex., *le pari* bet, wager, *le vélo* bicycle, *le menu* menu

4. Nouns ending in *-ment, -age, -ege* (note that *-age* and *-ege* end in "mute" *e)*. Ex., *le ménage* household, *le manège* riding school, *le document* document, *l'usage* usage
5. Names of days, months, seasons, metals, colors, trees, shrubs. Ex.:

le jeudi Thursday	*le bleu* blue
(le) septembre September	*le chêne* oak
le printemps spring	*l'olivier* olive tree
l'or gold	*le genêt* broom (a shrub)
le plomb lead	

6. The names of parts of speech when used as nouns. Ex., *le nom* noun, *le verbe* verb, *le participe* participle
7. Decimal weights and measures. Ex., *le mètre* meter, *le litre* liter, *le kilogramme* kilogram. Note the contrast with a nondecimal measure: *la livre* pound
8. The names of the cardinal points. Ex., *le nord* north, *l'est* east, *le sud* south, *l'ouest* west.

The following classes of nouns are generally feminine:

1. Nouns naming a female person. Ex., *la mère* mother, *la reine* queen.
   But: *le professeur* teacher (m. or f.)
2. Nouns ending in *-te, -son, -ion*. Ex., *la détente* détente, *la raison* reason, *la conversation* conversation
   But: *le camion* truck, *l'avion* airplane, *le million* million
3. Names of qualities or states of being ending in:

-nce	*la distance* distance
-esse	*la gentilesse* niceness
-eur	*la eur* width
	la douceur sweetness

But: *le bonheur* happiness, *le malheur* unhappiness, pain

-ude *la gratitude* gratitude

4. Most nouns ending in mute *e*. Ex., *la blague* joke, *la voiture* car
   But: See exceptions mentioned in item 4, page 283, under nouns of masculine gender.
5. Names of moral qualities, sciences, and arts.
   Ex., moral qualities: *la bonté* kindness, *l'avarice* greed
   science: *l'algèbra* algebra, *la chimie* chemistry
   art: *la peinture* painting, *la musique* music
   But: *l'art* (m.), art
6. Most names of fruits. Ex., *la pomme* apple, *la cerise* cherry
   But: *le pamplemousse* grapefruit, *le raisin* grapes
7. Nouns ending in -té (very few exceptions, if any). Ex., *l'activité* activity, *la générosité* generosity, *la proximité* proximity, *la priorité* priority

11. PLURAL OF NOUNS

1. Most nouns add *-s* to form the plural:

la ville	the city	*les villes*	the cities
l'île	the island	*les îles*	the islands

2. Nouns ending in *-s, -x, -z* do not change:

le fils	the son	*les fils*	the sons
la voix	the voice	*les voix*	the voices
le nez	the nose	*les nez*	the noses

3. Nouns ending in *-au* or *-eu* add *-x:*

le chapeau	the hat	*les chapeaux*	the hats

l'eau	water	*les eaux*	waters
le jeu	the game	*les jeux*	the games

4. Nouns ending in *-al* and *-ail* for the plural with *-aux*.

l'hôpital	the hospital	*les hôpitaux*	the hospitals
le travail	work	*les travaux*	works

Some Irregular Plurals:

le ciel	the sky	*les cieux*	the heavens
l'œil	the eye	*les yeux*	the eyes

12. FEMININE OF ADJECTIVES

1. The feminine of adjectives is normally formed by adding *-e* to the masculine singular, but if the masculine singular already ends in *-e*, the adjective has the same form in the feminine:

MASCULINE

un petit garçon	a little boy
un jeune homme	a young man

FEMININE

une petite fille	a little girl
une jeune femme	a young woman

2. Adjectives ending in *-er* change the *e* to *è* and then add *-e:*

étranger m.	*étrangère f.*	foreign

3. Adjectives ending in *-eux* change this ending to *-euse:*

heureux m.	*heureuse f.*	happy
sérieux m.	*sérieuse f.*	serious

4. Some adjectives double the final consonant and add *-e:*

bon m.	*bonne f.*	good
ancien m.	*ancienne f.*	former, ancient
gros m.	*grosse f.*	fat

5. There are a number of irregular feminines:

blanc m.	*blanche f.*	white
doux m.	*douce f.*	sweet, gentle, soft
faux m.	*fausse f.*	false
actif m.	*active f.*	active

13. PLURAL OF ADJECTIVES

1. The plural of adjectives is regularly formed by adding *-s* to the singular, but if the masculine singular ends in *-s* or *-x,* the masculine plural has the same form:

SINGULAR	PLURAL
un petit garçon a little boy	*deux petits garçons* two little boys
une petite fille a little girl	*deux petites filles* two little girls
un mauvais garçon a bad boy	*deux mauvais garçons* two bad boys

2. Adjectives ending in *-au* add *-x:*

un nouveau livre a new book	*de nouveaux livres* new books

3. Adjectives ending in *-al* change to *-aux*:

un homme loyal a loyal man	*des hommes loyaux* loyal men

14. AGREEMENT OF ADJECTIVES

1. Adjectives agree with the nouns they modify in gender and number; that is, they are masculine if the noun is masculine, plural if the noun is plural, etc.:

Marie et sa soeur sont petites.	Mary and her sister are little.

2. An adjective that modifies nouns of different gender is in the masculine plural:

Marie et Jean sont petits.	Mary and John are little.

15. POSITION OF ADJECTIVES

1. Adjectives usually follow the noun:

un livre français	a French book
un homme intéressant	an interesting man
une idée excellente	an excellent idea

2. When they describe an inherent quality or when they form a set phrase, etc., they precede the noun:

une jeune fille	a young girl
le savant auteur	the learned scholar
une étroite amitié	a close friendship
une éclatante victoire	a striking victory

3. The following common adjectives usually precede the nouns they modify:

autre	other	*jeune*	young
beau	beautiful	*joli*	pretty
bon	good	*long*	long
court	short	*mauvais*	bad
gentil	nice, pleasant	*nouveau*	new

grand	great, large, tall	*petit*	small, little
gros	big, fat	*vieux*	old

4. The following common adjectives differ in meaning depending on whether they come before or after the noun.

	BEFORE THE NOUN	AFTER THE NOUN
ancien	former	ancient
grand	great	tall
brave	worthy	brave
cher	dear (beloved)	dear (expensive)
pauvre	poor (wretched)	poor (indigent)
propre	own	clean
même	same	himself, herself itself, very

5. The following adjectives have two forms for the masculine singular:

MASCULINE SINGULAR		FEMININE SINGULAR	
Before a consonant	Before a vowel or "mute" *h*		
beau	*bel*	*belle*	beautiful, fine, handsome
nouveau	*nouvel*	*nouvelle*	new
vieux	*vieil*	*vieille*	old

Examples:

un beau livre	a beautiful book
un bel arbre	a beautiful tree
une belle femme	a beautiful woman

16. COMPARISON OF ADJECTIVES

Most adjectives form the comparative and superlative by placing *plus* and *le plus (la plus)* before the adjective:

POSITIVE	
petit	small
grand	large
COMPARATIVE	
plus petit	smaller
plus grand	larger
SUPERLATIVE	
le plus petit	the smallest
le plus grand	the largest

Common exceptions:

POSITIVE	
bon	good
mauvais	bad
COMPARATIVE	
meilleur	better
plus mauvais / *pire*	worse
SUPERLATIVE	
le meilleur	the best
le plus mauvais / *le pire*	the worst

17. POSSESSIVE ADJECTIVES

1. Possessive adjectives agree in gender and number with the thing possessed:

BEFORE SINGULAR NOUNS:		BEFORE PLURAL NOUNS:	
MASCULINE	FEMININE	MASCULINE AND FEMININE	
mon	*ma*	*mes*	my
ton	*ta*	*tes*	your (*fam.*)
son	*sa*	*ses*	his, her, its
notre	*notre*	*nos*	our
votre	*votre*	*vos*	your
leur	*leur*	*leurs*	their

Examples:

mon chien	my dog
sa mère	his (or her) mother
ma robe	my dress
votre livre	your book
leurs crayons	their pencils

2. Notice that these adjectives agree in gender not with the possessor as in English, but with the noun they modify. *Son, sa* and *ses* may therefore mean "his," "her," or "its.":

Jean parle à sa mère.	John is talking to his mother.
Marie parle à son père.	Mary is talking to her father.

3. Possessive adjectives are repeated before each noun they modify:

mon père et ma mère	my father and mother
leurs livres et leurs plumes	their books and pens

4. Before a feminine word beginning with a vowel or "mute" *h*, the forms *mon, ton, son* are used instead of *ma, ta, sa:*

son histoire	his story, his history
son école	his (or her) school

5. In speaking of parts of the body, the definite article is usually used instead of the possessive adjective (except where it might be ambiguous):

J'ai mal à la tête.	I have a headache.

18. POSSESSIVE PRONOUNS

MASCULINE		FEMININE		
Singular	Plural	Singular	Plural	
le mien	*les miens*	*la mienne*	*les miennes*	mine
le tien	*les tiens*	*la tienne*	*les tiennes*	your (fam.)
le sien	*les siens*	*la sienne*	*les siennes*	his, hers, its
le nôtre	*les nôtres*	*la nôtre*	*les nôtres*	ours
le vôtre	*les vôtres*	*la vôtre*	*les vôtres*	yours
le leur	*les leurs*	*la leur*	*les leurs*	theirs

Examples:

Voici le mien.	Here's mine.
Quel est la vôtre?	Which is yours? (fem. sing.)
Apportez les vôtres; j'apporterai les miens.	Bring yours; I'll bring mine.
J'ai mal à la tète.	I have a headache.

19. DEMONSTRATIVE ADJECTIVES

MASCULINE SINGULAR

ce (before a consonant)	*ce livre*	this (that) book
cet (before a vowel or "mute" *h*)	*cet arbre* *cet homme*	this (that) tree this (that) man

FEMININE SINGULAR

cette	*cette femme*	this (that) woman

PLURAL

ces	*ces hommes* *ces femmes*	these (those) men these (those) women

1. The demonstrative adjectives agree with the nouns they modify in gender and number. They must be repeated before each noun:

cet homme et cette femme	this man and this woman

2. The demonstrative adjective in French stands for both "this" and "that" (plural "these" and "those"). When it is necessary to distinguish between "this" and "that," *-ci* and *-là* are added to the noun.

Donnez-moi ce livre-ci.	Give me this book.
Voulez-vous cette robe-là?	Do you want that dress (over there)?
J'aime ce livre-ci mais je n'aime pas ce livre-là.	I like this book but I don't like that book.

20. DEMONSTRATIVE PRONOUNS

Masculine Singular	*celui*	this one, that one, the one
Feminine Singular	*celle*	this one, that one, the one
Masculine Plural	*ceux*	these, those, the ones
Feminine Plural	*celles*	these, those, the ones

Examples:

J'aime celui-ci.	I like that one.
Donnes-moi celle de ton frère.	Give me your brother's (pen, for example).

21. PERSONAL PRONOUNS

The forms of the pronouns will depend on whether they are:

1. the subject of a verb
2. the direct object of a verb
3. the indirect object of a verb
4. the object of a preposition
5. used as a reflexive pronoun
6. used in affirmative requests or commands

1. As the subject of a verb:

je	I
tu	you (fam.)
il	he, it
elle	she, it
nous	we
vous	you
ils	they
elles	they

a. *Vous* is the pronoun normally used in talking to one person or several perople. *Tu* is used in addressing people you know very well (whom you call by their first name in English

—a member of one's family or a close friend; also children, pets, etc.).

b. *Il, elle, ils* and *elles* are used as pronouns referring to things as well as to persons. They have the same number and gender as the nouns to which they refer. *Ils* is used to refer to nouns of different genders:

Où est le livre?	Where's the book?
Il est sur la table.	It's on the table.
Où est la lettre?	Where's the letter?
Elle est sur la table.	It's on the table.
Où sont les livres et les lettres?	Where are the books and letters?
Ils sont sur la table.	They're on the table.

2. As the direct object of a verb:

me	me
te	you
le	him, it
la	her, it
nous	us
vous	you
les	them
en	some, any

3. As the indirect object of a verb:

me	to me
te	to you
lui	to him, to her
nous	to us
vous	to you
leur	to them
y	to it, there

4. As the object of a preposition:

moi	I, me
toi	you (fam.)
soi	himself, oneself
lui	he, him

elle	she, her
nous	we, us
vous	you
eux	they, them (masc.)
elles	they, them (fem.)

5. As a reflexive pronoun:

me	myself
te	yourself
se	himself, herself, itself, oneself
nous	ourselves
vous	yourself, yourselves
se	themselves

6. In affirmative requests and commands:

Direct Object		*Indirect Object*	
le *la* *les*	before	*moi/toi*[1] *nous* *vous* *lui* *leur*	before *y* before *en*

22. POSITION OF PRONOUNS

The direct and indirect pronoun objects generally precede the verb except in affirmative commands and requests.

[1] When *moi* or *toi* are used with *en*, they become *m'* and *t'* and precede *en*.

Examples: Donnez-*le-moi*. BUT: Donnez-*m'en*.
Lève-*toi* BUT: Va-t'en.

1. Position before a verb:

me, *te*, *se*, *nous*, *vous*	come before	*le*, *la*, *les*	before	*lui*	before *y*
				leur	before *en*

Examples:

Il me le donne.	He gives it to me.
Il le lui donne.	He gives it to him (to her, to it).
Je l'y ai vu.	I saw him there.
Je leur en parlerai.	I'll speak to them about it.

2. Position after a verb:

le, *la*, *les*	come before	*me* (moi), *te* (toi), *lui*, *nous*, *vous*, *leur*	before *y*	before *en*

Examples:

Donnez-le-lui.	Give it to him.
Donnez-leur-en.	Give them some.
Allez-vous-en.	Go away. Get out of here.

3. In affirmative commands, both the direct and indirect object pronoun follow the verb, the direct preceding the indirect:

Donnez-moi-le livre.	Give me the book.
Donnez-le-moi.	Give it to me.
Montrez-moi les pommes.	Show me the apples.
Montrez-m'en.	Show me some.
Ecrivez-lui une lettre.	Write him a letter.
Ecrivez-la-lui.	Write it to him.

4. The pronoun objects precede *voici* and *voilà:*

Où est le livre?	Where's the book?
Le voici.	Here it is.

23. RELATIVE PRONOUNS

1. As the subject of a verb:

qui	who, which, that
ce qui	what, that which

2. As the object of a verb:

que	whom, which, that
ce que	what, that which

3. As the object of a preposition:

qui (for a person)	whom
lequel (for a thing)	which

Note: *dont* means whose, of whom, of which:

le problème dont je connais la solution. . .	The problem whose solution I know. . .
Le professeur dont je vous ai parlè. . .	The teacher about whom I talked to you. . .

24. INDEFINITE PRONOUNS

quelque chose	something
quelqu'un	someone
chacun	each (one)
on	one, people, they, etc.
ne . . . rien	nothing
ne . . . personne	no one

25. NOUN USED AS INDIRECT OBJECT

A noun used as an indirect object is always preceded by the preposition *à*.

Je donne un livre à la jeune fille.	I'm giving the girl a book.

26. REPETITION OF PREPOSITIONS

The prepositions *à* and *de* must be repeated before each of their objects:

Je parle au deputé et à son secrétaire.	I'm speaking to the deputy and his secretary.
Voici les cahiers de Jean et ceux de Marie.	Here are John's and Mary's notebooks.

27. THE PARTITIVE

1. When a noun is used in such a way as to express or imply quantity, it is preceded by the article with *de*. This construction very often translates the English "some" or "a few."

J'ai de l'argent.	I have some money.
Il a des amis.	He has a few friends.

In many cases, however, the article is used where we don't use "some" or "a few" in English:

A-t-il des amis ici?	Does he have friends here?

2. The article is omitted:

a. When an expression of quantity is used:

J'ai beaucoup d'argent.	I have a lot of money.
Combien de livres avez-vous?	How many books do you have?

Exceptions: *bien* much,many, and *la plupart* most, the majority:

bien des hommes	many men
le plupart des hommes	most men

b. When the noun is preceded by an adjective:

J'ai acheté de belles cravates.	I bought some nice ties.

c. When the sentence is negative:

Il n'a pas d'amis.	He has no friends.
Mon ami n'a pas d'argent.	My friend hasn't any money.

28. NEGATION

A sentence is made negative by placing *ne* before the verb and *pas* after it:

Je sais.	I know.
Je ne sais pas.	I don't know.
Je ne l'ai pas vu.	I haven't seen it.

Other negative expressions:

ne . . . guère	hardly
ne . . . point	not (at all)
ne . . . rien	nothing
ne . . . nul, nulle	no one, no
ne . . . jamais	never
ne . . . personne	nobody
ne . . . plus	no longer
ne . . . ni . . . ni	neither . . nor
ne . . . que	only
ne . . . aucun, aucune	no one

29. WORD ORDER IN QUESTIONS

1. Questions with pronoun subjects:

There are two ways of asking a question with a pronoun subject:

a. Place the pronoun after the verb:

Parlez-vous français?	Do you speak French?

b. Place *est-ce que* ("is it that") before the sentence[1]:

Est-ce que je parle trop vite?	Am I talking too fast?
Est-ce que vous parlez français?	Do you speak French?

2. Questions with noun subjects:

When a question begins with a noun, the pronoun is repeated after the verb:

Votre frère parle-t-il français?	Does your brother speak French?
Votre soeur a-t-elle quitté la maison?	Has your sister left the house?

3. Questions introduced by interrogative words:

In questions which begin with an interrogative word *(quand, comment, où, pourquoi),* the order is usually interrogative word—noun subject—verb—personal pronoun:

Pourquoi votre ami a-t-il quitté Paris?	Why did your friend leave Paris?

30. ADVERBS

1. Most adverbs are formed from the adjectives by adding *-ment* to the feminine form:

froid	cold	*froidement*	coldly
certain	certain	*certainement*	certainly
naturel	natural	*naturellement*	naturally
facile	easy	*facilement*	easily

2. There are many irregular adverbs which must be learned separately:

[1] In the first person singular this is the usual way of asking a question.

vite	quickly	*mal*	badly

3. Adverbs are compared like adjectives (see page 287):

POSITIVE		COMPARATIVE		SUPERLATIVE	
loin	far	*plus loin*	farther	*le plus loin*	the farthest

4. Some common adverbs of place:

ici	here
là	there
à côté	at the side
de côté	aside
devant	before, in front of
derrière	behind
dessus	on top
dessous	underneath
dedans	inside
dehors	outside
partout	everywhere
nulle part	nowhere
loin	far
près	near
où	where
y	there
ailleurs	elsewhere
là-haut	up there
là-bas	over there

5. Some common adverbs of time:

aujourd'hui	today
demain	tomorrow
hier	yesterday
avant-hier	the day before yesterday
après-demain	the day after tomorrow
maintenant	now
alors	then

avant	before
autrefois	once, formerly
jadis	once, formerly
tôt	early
bientôt	soon
tard	late
souvent	often
ne . . . jamais	never
toujours	always, ever
longtemps	long, for a long time
tantôt	soon, presently
tantôt . . . tantôt	now . . . now, sometimes . . . sometimes
encore	still, yet
ne . . . plus	no longer, no more

6. Adverbs of manner:

bien	well
mal	ill, badly
ainsi	thus, so
de même	similarly
autrement	otherwise
ensemble	together
fort	much, very
volontiers	willingly
surtout	above all, especially
exprès	on purpose, expressly

7. Adverbs of quantity or degree:

beaucoup	much, many
assez	enough
ne . . . guère	not much, scarcely
peu	little
plus	more
ne . . . plus	no more
moins	less
encore	more
bien	much, many

trop	too, too much, too many
tellement	so much, so many

31. THE INFINITIVE

The commonest endings of the infinitive are:

I	-*er parler*	to speak	(The First Conjugation)
II	-*ir finir*	to finish	(The Second Conjugation)
III	-*re vendre*	to sell	(The Third Conjugation)

32. THE PAST PARTICIPLE

1. Forms:

	INFINITIVE	PAST PARTICIPLE
I	*parler*	*parl-é*
II	*finir*	*fin-i*
III	*perdre*	*perd-u*

2. Agreement:
   a. When a verb is conjugated with *avoir*, the past participle agrees in gender and number with the preceding direct object:

La pièce que j'ai vue hier était mauvaise.	The play I saw yesterday was bad.
Avez-vous vu le livre qu'il a acheté?	Have you seen the book he bought?
Avez-vous donné la plume à Charles?	Did you give the pen to Charles?
Non, je l'ai donnée à Claire.	No, I gave it to Claire.

   b. In the case of reflexive verbs the past participle agrees with the reflexive direct object:

Ils se sont levés.	They got up.
Elle s'est lavée.	She washed herself.

c. In the case of intransitive verbs conjugated with *être,* the past participle agrees with the subject:

Marie est arrivée hier.	Mary arrived yesterday.
Jean et Pierre se sont levés.	John and Peter got up.
Ils sont arrivés.	They arrived.
Nous sommes rentrés trés tard.	We came back very late.

33. THE INDICATIVE

SIMPLE TENSES

1. The present tense is formed by the verb stem plus the endings *-e, -es, -e, -ons, -ez, -ent*. It has several English translations:

je parle	I speak, I am speaking I do speak
ils mangent	They eat, they are eating, they do eat

2. The imperfect tense is formed by dropping the *-ant* of the present participle and adding *-ais, -ais, -ait, -ions, -iez, -aient*. It expresses a continued or habitual action in the past. It also indicates an action that was happening when something else happened:

Je me levais à sept heures.	I used to get up at seven o'clock.
Il dormait quand Jean est entré.	He was sleeping when John entered.
Il parlait souvent de cela.	He often spoke about that.

Il faisait nuit quand il est sorti. — It was night when he went out.

3. The future tense is formed by adding to the infinitive or future stem the endings, *-ai, -as, -a, -ons, -ez, -ont*. It indicates a future action:

Il arrivera demain. — He'll arrive tomorrow.
Je le vendrai demain. — I'll sell it tomorrow.

4. The past definite tense is formed by adding to the root the endings *-ai, -as, -a, -âmes, -âtes, -èrent* for *-er* verbs; the endings *-is, -is, -it, -îmes, -îtes, -irent* for *-ir* verbs; and for all other verbs either these last or *-us, -us, -ut, -ûmes, -ûtes, -urent*. It expresses an action begun and ended in the past, and it is not generally used in the first person. This tense is used in formal narrative; in conversation and informal writing, the past indefinite tense (see below) is used:

Le roi fut rué. — The king was killed.
Les soldats entrèrent dans la ville. — The soldiers entered the city.

5. The past indefinite tense or "conversational past" is formed by adding the past participle to the present indicative of *avoir* or, in a few cases, *être*. It is used to indicate a past action which has been completed.

Il ne m'a rien dit. — He didn't tell me anything.
J'ai fini mon travail. — I finished my work. I have finished my work.
L'avez vous vu? — Have you seen him? Did you see him?

Ils sont arrivés. They arrived.

6. The past perfect tense is formed by adding the past participle to the imperfect of *avoir* or, in a few cases, *être*. It translates the English past perfect:

Il l'avait fait. He had done it.
Lorsque je revins, il était parti. When I came back, he had gone.

7. The past anterior tense is formed by adding the past participle to the past definite of *avoir* or, in a few cases, *être*. It is used for an event that happened just before another event. It is rarely found except after *quand* and *lorsque* "when," *après que* "after," *dès que* "as soon as." It is used only in literary style.

Après qu'il eut dîné il sortit. As soon as he had eaten, he went out.
Quand il eut fini il se leva. When he had finished, he got up.

8. The future perfect tense is formed by adding the past participle to the future of *avoir* or, in a few cases, *être*. It translates the English future perfect:

Il aura bientôt fini. He will soon have finished.

Sometimes it indicates probability:

Il le lui aura sans doute dit. No doubt he must have told him.
Il aura été malade. He probably was sick.
Je me serai trompé. I must have been mistaken.

9. The most common intransitive verbs which are conjugated with the verb *être* in the compound tenses are the following:

aller, arriver, descendre, entrer, monter, mourir,

naître, partir, rester, retourner, sortir, tomber, venir, revenir.

Examples:

Je suis venu.	I have come.
Il est arrivé.	He has arrived.
Nous sommes partis.	We have left.

10. Reflexive verbs are conjugated with the auxiliary *être* in the past indefinite:

Je me suis lavé les mains.	I have washed my hands.
Je me suis levé à sept heures ce matin.	I got up at seven o'clock this morning.

CONDITIONAL

1. The conditional is formed by adding to the infinitive the endings *-ais, -ais, -ait, -ions, -iez, -aient*. It translates English "would" or "should":

Je le prendrais si j'étais à votre place.	I would take it if I were you.
Je ne ferais jamais une chose pareille.	I would never do such a thing.

2. The conditional perfect if formed by adding the past participle to the conditional of *avoir* or, in a few cases, *être*. It translates the English "if I had" or "if I would have," etc.:

Si j'avais su, je n'y serais jamais allé.	If I had (would have) known, I should never have gone there.
Si j'avais eu assez d'argent je l'aurais acheté.	If I had (would have had) the money, I would have bought it.

34. THE IMPERATIVE

1. The imperative of most verbs is generally formed from the present indicative tense. (In the verbs of the first conjugation, however, the second person singular loses the final *s*):

donner	to give	*finir*	to finish
donne (fam.)	give	*finis* (fam.)	finish
donnez	give	*finissez*	finish
donnons	let us give	*finissons*	let us finish

vendre	to sell
vends (fam.)	sell
vendez	sell
vendons	let us sell

2. Imperatives of *être* and *avoir:*

être	to be	*avoir*	to have
sois (fam.)	be	*aie* (fam.)	have
soyez	be	*ayez*	have
soyons	let us be	*ayons*	let us have

35. VERBS FOLLOWED BY THE INFINITIVE

1. Some verbs are followed by the inifinitive without a preceding preposition:

Je vais parler à Jean.	I am going to talk to John.
J'aime parler français.	I like to speak French.
Je ne sais pas danser.	I don't know how to dance.

2. Some verbs are followed by *à* plus the infinitive:

J'apprends à parler français.	I am learning to speak French.
Je l'aiderai à le faire.	I'll help him do it.

3. Some verbs are followed by *de* plus the infinitive:

Il leur a demandè de fermer la porte.	He asked them to shut the door.

36. THE SUBJUNCTIVE

The indicative makes a simple statement; the subjunctive indicates a certain attitude toward the statement—uncertainty, desire, emotion, etc. The subjunctive is used in subordinate clauses when the statement is unreal, doubtful, indefinite, subject to some condition, or is affected by will, emotion, etc.

FORMS

1. Present Subjunctive:

Drop the *-ent* of the third person plural present indicative and add *-e, -es, -e, -ions, -iez, -ient*. See the forms of the regular subjunctive in the Regular Verb Charts.

The irregular verbs *avoir* and *être:*

que j'aie	*que je sois*
que tu aies	*que tu sois*
qu'il ait	*qu'il soit*
que nous ayons	*que nous soyons*
que vous ayez	*que vous soyez*
qu'ils aient	*qu'ils soient*

2. Imperfect Subjunctive:

Drop the ending of the first person singular of the past definite and add *-sse, -sses, -t,*

-ssions, -ssiez, -ssent, putting a circumflex over the last vowel of the third person singular:

(that) I gave, might give	(that) I finished, might finish
que je donnasse	*que je finisse*
que tu donnasses	*que tu finisses*
qu'il donnât	*qu'il finît*
que nous donnassions	*que nous finissions*
que vous donnassiez	*que nous finnissiez*
qu'ils donnassent	*qu'ils finissent*

(that) I sold, might sell

que je vendisse
que tu vendisses
qu'il vendît
que nous vendissions
que vous vendissiez
qu'ils vendissent

3. Perfect Subjunctive:

   Add the past participle to the present subjunctive of *avoir* (or, in a few cases, *être):*

   avoir: que j'aie donné, que tu aies donné, etc.
   être: que je sois allé, que tu sois allé, etc.

4. Pluperfect Subjunctive:

   Add the past participle to the imperfect subjunctive of *avoir* (or, in a few cases, *être):*

   avoir: j'eusse donné, etc.
   être: je fusse allé, etc.

USES

1. After verbs of command, request, permission, etc.:

Je tiens à ce que vous y alliez.	I insist on your going there.

2. After expressions of approval and disapproval, necessity, etc.:

Il n'est que juste que vous le lui disiez.	It's only fair that you tell him that.
Il faut que vous fassiez cela.	You have to do that.

3. After verbs of emotion (desire, regret, fear, joy, etc.):

Je voudrais bien que vous veniez avec nous.	I'd like you to come with us.
Je regrette que vous ne puissiez pas venir.	I'm sorry you can't come.

4. After expressions of doubt, uncertainty, denial:

Je doute que j'y aille.	I doubt that I'll go there.
Il est possible qu'il ne puisse pas venir.	It's possible that he may not be able to come.

5. In relative clauses with an indefinite antecedent:

Il me faut quelqu'un qui fasse cela.	I need someone to do that.

6. In adverbial clauses after certain conjunctions denoting purpose, time, concession, etc.:

Je viendrai à moins qu'il ne pleuve.	I'll come unless it rains.
Asseyez-vous en attendant que ce soit prêt.	Sit down until it's ready.

7. In utterances expressing a wish or command:

Qu'ils s'en aillent!	Let them go away!
Dieu vous bénisse!	God bless you!
Vive la France!	Long live France!

VERB CHARTS

I. FORMS OF THE REGULAR VERBS

A. CLASSES I, II, III

Infinitive	Pres. & Past Participles	Present Indicative	Present Subjunctive†	Conversational Past	Past Subjunctive	Imperfect Indicative
-er ending	parlant	parl + e	parl + e	j'ai + parlé	que j'aie + parlé	parl + ais
parler	parlé	es	es	tu as	que tu aies	ais
		e	e	il a	qu'il ait	ait
		ons	ions	nou avons	que nous ayons	ions
		ez	iez	vous avez	que vous ayez	iez
		ent	ent	ils ont	qu'ils aient	aient
-ir ending	finissant	fin + is	finiss + e	j'ai + fini	que j'aie + fini	finiss + ais
finir	fini	is	es	tu as	que tu aies	ais
		it	e	il a	qu'il ait	ait
		issons	ions	nous avons	que nous ayons	ions
		issez	iez	vous avez	que vous ayez	iez
		issent	ent	ils ont	qu'ils aient	aient
-re ending	vendant	vend + s	vend + e	j'ai + vendu	que j'aie + vendu	vend + ais
vendre	vendu	s	es	tu as	que tu aies	ais
		—	e	il a	qu'il ait	ait
		ons	ions	nous avons	que nous ayons	ions
		ez	iez	vous avez	que vous ayez	iez
		ent	ent	ils ont	qu'ils aient	aient

† Like the past subjunctive, the present subjunctive verb is always preceded by *que* or *qu'* + the appropriate pronoun, as in "*Il faut que je parte*" and "*Je veux que quitte la maison.*"

Past Perfect	Future	Future Perfect	Conditional	Conditional Perfect	Imperative
j'avais + parlé	parler + ai	j'aurai + parlé	parler + ais	j'aurais + parlé	
tu avais	as	tu auras	ais	tu aurais	parle
il avait	a	il aura	ait	il aurait	
nous avions	ons	nous aurons	ions	nous aurions	parlons
vous aviez	ez	vous aurez	iez	vous auriez	parlez
ils avaient	ont	ils auront	aient	ils auraient	
j'avais + fini	finir + ai	j'aurai + fini	finir + ais	j'aurais + fini	
tu avais	as	tu auras	ais	tu aurais	finis
il avait	a	il aura	ait	il aurait	
nous avions	ons	nous aurons	ions	nous aurions	finissons
vous aviez	ez	vous aurez	iez	vous auriez	finissez
ils avaient	ont	ils auront	aient	il auraient	
j'avais + vendu	vendr + ai	j'aurai + vendu	vendr + ais	j'aurais + vendu	
tu avais	as	tu auras	ais	tu aurais	vends
il avait	a	il aura	ait	il aurait	
nous avions	ons	nous aurons	ions	nous aurions	vendons
vous aviez	ez	vous aurez	iez	vous auriez	vendez
ils avaient	ont	ils auront	aient	ils auraient	

B. VERBS ENDING IN *-CER* AND *-GER*

Infinitive	Pres. & Past Participles	Present Indicative	Present Subjunctive	Conversational Past	Past Subjunctive	Imperfect Indicative
[1] **placer**	*plaçant*	place	place	j'ai + placé	que j'aie + placé	*plaçais*
	placé	places	places	tu as	que tu aies	*plaçais*
		place	place	il a	qu'il ait	*plaçait*
		plaçons	placions	nous avons	que nous ayons	placions
		placez	placiez	vous avez	que vous ayez	placiez
		placent	placent	ils ont	qu'ils aient	*plaçaient*
[2] **manger**	*mangeant*	mange	mange	j'ai + mangé	que j'aie + mangé	*mangeais*
	mangé	manges	manges	tu as	que tu aies	*mangeais*
		mange	mange	il a	qu'il ait	*mangeait*
		mangeons	mangions	nous avons	que nous ayons	mangions
		mangez	mangiez	vous avez	que vous ayez	mangiez
		mangent	mangent	ils ont	qu'ils aient	*mangeaient*

[1] Similarly conjugated: *commencer, lancer, etc.*

[2] Similarly conjugated: *plonger, ranger, arranger*, etc.

Past Perfect	Future	Future Perfect	Conditional	Conditional Perfect	Imperative
j'avais + placé	placer + ai	j'aurai + placé	placer + ais	j'aurais + placé	
tu avais	as	tu auras	ais	tu aurais	place
il avait	a	il aura	ait	il aurait	
nous avions	ons	nous aurons	ions	nous aurions	*plaçons*
vous aviez	ez	vous aurez	iez	vous auriez	
ils avaient	ont	ils auront	aient	ils auraient	placez
j'avais + mangé	manger – ai	j'aurai + mangé	manger + ais	j'aurais + mangé	
tu avais	as	tu auras	ais	tu aurais	mange
il avait	a	il aura	ait	il aurait	
nous avions	ons	nous aurons	ions	nous aurions	*mangeons*
vous aviez	ez	vous aurez	iez	vous auriez	mangez
ils avaient	ont	ils auront	aient	il auraient	

C. VERBS ENDING IN *-ER* WITH CHANGES IN THE STEM

Infinitive	Pres. & Past Participles	Present Indicative	Present Subjunctive	Conversational Past	Past Subjunctive	Imperfect Indicative
[1] **acheter**	achetant	*achète*	*achète*	j'ai + acheté	que j'aie + acheté	achet + ais
	acheté	*achètes*	*achètes*	tu as	que tu aies	ais
		achète	*achètes*	il a	qu'il ait	ait
		achetons	achetions	nous avons	que nous ayons	ions
		achetez	achetiez	vous avez	que vous ayez	iez
		achètent	*achètent*	ils ont	qu'ils aient	aient
[2] **appeler**	appelant	*appelle*	*appelle*	j'ai + appelé	que j'aie + appelé	appel + ais
	appelé	*appelles*	*appelles*	tu as	que tu aies	ais
		appelle	*appelle*	il a	qu'il ait	ait
		appelons	appelions	nous avons	que nous ayons	ions
		appelez	appeliez	vous avez	que vous ayez	iez
		appellent	*appellent*	ils ont	qu'ils aient	aient
[3] **payer†**	payant	*paie*/paye	*paie*/paye	j'ai + payé	que j'aie + payé	pay + ais
	payé	*paies*/payes	*paies*/payes	tu as	que tu aies	ais
		paie/paye	*paie*/paye	il a	qu'il ait	ait
		payons	payions	nous avons	que nous ayons	ions
		payez	payiez	vous avez	que vous ayez	iez
		paient/payent	*paient*/payent	il ont	qu'ils aient	aient
[4] **préférer**	préférant	*préfère*	*préfère*	j'ai + préféré	que j'aie + préféré	préfér + ais
	préféré	*préfères*	*préfères*	tu as	que tu aies	ais
		préfère	*préfère*	il a	qu'il ait	ait
		préférons	préférions	nous avons	que nous ayons	ions
		préférez	préfériez	vous avez	que vous ayez	iez
		préfèrent	*préfèrent*	il ont	qu'ils aient	aient

[1] Verbs like *acheter: mener, amener, emmener, se promener, lever, se lever, élever*

[2] Verbs like *appeler: se rappeler, jeter*

[3] Verbs like *payer: essayer, employer, ennuyer, essuyer, nettoyer* (See note below.)

Past Perfect	Future	Future Perfect	Conditional	Conditional Perfect	Imperative
j'avais + acheté	*achèter* + ai	j'aurai + acheté	*achèter* + ais	j'aurais + acheté	
tu avais	as	tu auras	ais	tu aurais	*achète*
il avait	a	il aura	ait	il aurait	
nous avions	ons	nous aurons	ions	nous aurions	*achetons*
vous aviez	ez	vous aurez	iez	vous auriez	*achetez*
ils avaient	ont	ils auront	aient	ils auraient	
j'avais + appelé	*appeller* + ai	j'aurai + appelé	*appeller* + ais	j'aurais + appelé	
tu avais	as	tu auras	ais	tu aurais	*appelle*
il avait	a	il aura	ait	il aurait	
nous avions	ons	nous aurons	ions	nous aurions	appelons
vous aviez	ez	vous aurez	iez	vous auriez	appelez
ils avaient	ont	ils auront	aient	il auraient	
j'avais + payé	*paier* + ai	j'aurai + payé	*paier* + ais	j'aurais + payé	
tu avais	*or* as	tu auras	*or* ais	tu aurais	*paie*/paye
il avait	payer + a	il aura	payer + ait	il aurait	
nous avions	ons	nous aurons	ions	nous aurions	payons
vous aviez	ez	vous aurez	iez	vous auriez	payez
ils avaient	ont	ils auront	aient	ils auraient	
j'avais + préféré	préférer + ai	j'aurai + préféré	préférer + ais	j'aurais + préféré	
tu avais	as	tu auras	ais	tu aurais	*préfère*
il avait	a	il aura	ait	il aurait	
nous avions	ons	nous aurons	ions	nous aurions	préférons
vous aviez	ez	vous aurez	iez	vous auriez	préférez
ils avaient	ont	ils auront	aient	ils auraient	

(4) Verbs like *préférer: espérer, répéter, célébrer, considérer, suggérer, protéger*

† Verbs ending in *-ayer* may use *i* or *y* in the present (except for *nous* and *vous* forms), the future, and the conditional, as in *payer, essayer*. Verbs ending in *-oyer, -uyer* change *y* to *i* (as in *essuyer, ennuyer, employer, nettoyer*).

D. VERBS ENDING IN *-OIR*

Infinitive	Pres. & Past Participles	Present Indicative	Present Subjunctive	Conversational Past	Past Subjunctive	Imperfect Indicative
[1] **recevoir**	recevant	*reçois*	*reçoive*	j'ai + *reçu*	que j'aie + *reçu*	recev + ais
	reçu	*reçois*	*reçoives*	tu as	que tu aies	ais
		reçoit	*reçoive*	il a	qu'il ait	ait
		recevons	recevions	nou avons	que nous ayons	ions
		recevez	receviez	vous avez	que vous ayez	iez
		reçoivent	*reçoivent*	ils ont	qu'ils aient	aient

[1] Verbs like *recevoir: devoir, (dois, doive, dû)*

Past Perfect	Future	Future Perfect	Conditional	Conditional Perfect	Imperative
j'avais + *reçu*	recevr + ai	j'aurai + *reçu*	recevr + ais	j'aurais + *reçu*	
tu avais	as	tu auras	ais	tu aurais	*reçois*
il avait	a	il aura	ait	il aurait	
nous avions	ons	nous aurons	ions	nous aurions	recevons
vous aviez	ez	vous aurez	iez	vous auriez	recevez
ils avaient	ont	ils auront	aient	ils auraient	

E. VERBS ENDING IN *-NDRE*

Infinitive	Pres. & Past Participles	Present Indicative	Present Subjunctive	Conversational Past	Past Subjunctive	Imperfect Indicative
[2] **craindre**	*craignant*	*crains*	*craigne*	j'ai + *craint*	que j'aie + *craint*	*craign* + ais
	craint	*crains*	*craignes*	tu as	que tu aies	ais
		craint	*craigne*	il a	qu'il ait	ait
		craignons	*craignions*	nou avons	que nous ayons	ions
		craignez	*craigniez*	vous avez	que vous ayez	iez
		craignent	*craignent*	ils ont	qu'ils aient	aient
[3] **eteindre**	*éteignant*	*éteins*	*éteigne*	j'ai + *éteint*	que j'aie + *éteint*	*éteign* + ais
	éteint	*éteins*	*éteignes*	tu as	que tu aies	ais
		éteint	*éteigne*	il a	qu'il ait	ait
		éteignons	*éteignions*	nou avons	que nous ayons	ions
		étegnez	*éteigniez*	vous avez	que vous ayez	iez
		éteignent	*éteignent*	ils ont	qu'ils aient	aient

[2] Verbs like *craindre: plaindre*, to pity. The reflexive form, *se plaindre*, means "to complain," and in the compound tenses is conjugated with *être*.

[3] Verbs like *éteindre: peindre*, to paint; *teindre*, to dye.

Past Perfect	Future	Future Perfect	Conditional	Conditional Perfect	Imperative
j'avais + *craint*	craindr + ai	j'aurai + *craint*	craindr + ais	j'aurais + *craint*	*crains*
tu avais	as	tu auras	ais	tu aurais	
il avait	a	il aura	ait	il aurait	*craignons*
nous avions	ons	nous aurons	ions	nous aurions	*craignez*
vous aviez	ez	vous aurez	iez	vous auriez	
ils avaient	ont	ils auront	aient	ils auraient	
j'avais + *éteint*	éteindr + ai	j'aurai + *éteint*	éteindr + ais	j'aurais + *éteint*	*éteins*
tu avais	as	tu auras	ais	tu aurais	
il avait	a	il aura	ait	il aurait	*éteignons*
nous avions	ons	nous aurons	ions	nous aurions	*éteignez*
vous aviez	ez	vous aurez	iez	vous auriez	
ils avaient	ont	ils auront	aient	ils auraient	

F. COMPOUND TENSES OF VERBS CONJUGATED WITH *ÊTRE*

Conversational past	Past subjunctive	Past perfect	Future perfect	Conditional perfect
je suis allé(e)	que je sois allé(e)	j'étais allé(e)	je serai allé(e)	je serais allé(e)
tu es allé(e)	que tu sois allé(e)	tu étais allé(e)	tu seras allé(e)	tu serais allé(e)
il est allé	qu'il soit allé	il était allé	il sera allé	il serait allé
elle est allée	qu'elle soit allée	elle était allée	elle sera allée	elle serait allée
nous sommes allé(e)s	que nous soyons allé(e)s	nous étions allé(e)s	nous serons allé(e)s	nous serions allé(e)s
vous êtes allé(e)(s)	que vous soyez allé(e)(s)	vous étiez allé(e)(s)	vous serez allé(e)(s)	vous seriez allé(e)(s)
ils sont allés	qu'ils soient allés	ils étaient allés	ils seront allés	ils seraient allés
elles sont allées	qu'elles soient allées	elles étaient allées	elles seront allées	elles seraient allées

G. COMPOUND TENSES OF REFLEXIVE VERBS (ALL REFLEXIVE VERBS ARE CONJUGATED WITH *ÊTRE*).

Conversational past	Past subjunctive	Past perfect	Future perfect	Conditional perfect
je me suis levé(e)	que je me sois levé(e)	je m'étais levé(e)	je me serai levé(e)	je me serais levé(e)
tu t'es levé(e)	que tu te sois levé(e)	tu t'étais levé(e)	tu te seras levé(e)	tu te serais levé(e)
il s'est levé	qu'il se soit levé	il s'était levé	il se sera levé	il se serait levé
elle s'est levée	qu'elle se soit levée	elle s'était levée	elle se sera levée	elle se serait levée
nous nous sommes levé(e)s	que nous nous soyons levé(e)s	nous nous étions levé(e)s	nous nous serons levé(e)s	nous nous serions levé(e)s
vous vous êtes levé(e)(s)	que vous vous soyez levé(e)(s)	vous vous étiez levé(e)(s)	vous vous serez levé(e)(s)	vous vous seriez levé(e)(s)
ils se sont levés	qu'ils se soient levés	ils s'étaient levés	ils seront levés	ils se seraient levés
elles se sont levées	qu'elles se soient levées	elles s'étaient levées	elles seront levées	elles se seraient levées

H. INFREQUENTLY USED AND "LITERARY" TENSES (CLASSES I, II, III)

(1) Past Definite†			(2) Past Anterior			(3) Imperfect Subjunctive		
parlai	finis	perdis	eus parlé	eus fini	eus perdu	parlasse	finisse	perdisse
parlas	finis	perdis	eus parlé	eus fini	eus perdu	parlasses	finisses	perdisses
parla	finit	perdit	eut parlé	eut fini	eut perdu	parlât	finît	perdit
parlâmes	finîmes	perdîmes	eûmes parlé	eûmes fini	eûmes perdu	parlassions	finissions	perdissions
parlâtes	finîtes	perdîtes	eûtes parlé	eûtes fini	eûtes perdu	parlassiez	finissiez	perdissiez
parlèrent	finirent	perdirent	eurent parlé	eurent fini	eurent perdu	parlassent	finissent	perdissent

(1) Used in formal narrative only. In informal conversation and writing, use the conversational past (*j'ai parlé*, etc.)

(2) Used, in literary style only, after *quand, lorsque, après que, dès que* for an event that happened just before another event. Example: *Après qu'il eut diné il sortit*. As soon as he had eaten, he went out.

(3) "that I spoke," "that I might speak," etc. This tense is infrequently found in ordinary conversation, but is used fairly often in literary works.

† All other regular verbs use either the *-er, -ir,* or *-re* endings, depending upon the conjugation to which they belong. The past definite forms of irregular verbs must be memorized.

(4) Past Perfect Subjunctive		
que j'eusse parlé	que j'eusse fini	que j'eusse perdu
que tu eusses parlé	que tu eusses fini	que tu eusses perdu
qu'il eût parlé	qu'il eût fini	qu'il eût perdu
que nous eussions parlé	que nous eussion fini	que nous eussions perdu
que vous eussiez parlé	que vous eussiez fini	que vous eussiez perdu
qu'ils eussent parlé	qu'ils eussent fini	qu'ils eussent perdu

(4) "that I had spoken," that I might have spoken," etc. A predominantly literary tense.

II. FREQUENTLY USED IRREGULAR VERBS

(1) The correct auxiliary verb is indicated in parentheses below each verb.
(2) For compound tenses, use the appropriate form of the auxiliary verb + past participle.

Infinitive	Pres. & Past Participles	Present Indicative	Present Subjunctive	Imperfect Indicative	Future	Conditional	Imperative
acquérir	acquériant	acquiers	acquière	acquér + ais	acquerr + ai	acquerr + ais	
to acquire	acquis	acquiers	acquières	ais	as	ais	acquiers
(avoir)		acquiert	acquière	ait	a	ait	
		acquérons	acquérions	ions	ons	ions	acquérons
		acquérez	acquériez	iez	ez	iez	acquérez
		acquièrent	acquièrent	aient	ont	aient	
aller	allant	vais	aille	all + ais	ir + ai	ir + ais	
to go	allé(e)(s)	vas	ailles	ais	as	ais	va
(être)		va	aille	ait	a	ait	
		allons	allions	ions	ons	ions	allons
		allez	alliez	iez	ez	iez	allez
		vont	aillent	aient	ont	aient	
(s')asseoir†	asseyant	assieds	asseye	assey + ais	asseyer + ai	asseyer + ais	
to sit (down)	assie(e)(s)	assieds	asseyes	ais	*or* as	*or* ais	assieds-toi
(être)		assied	asseye	ait	assiér + a	assiér + ait	
		asseyons	asseyions	ions	*or* ons	*or* ions	asseyons-nous
		asseyez	asseyiez	iez	assoir + ez	assoir + iez	asseyez-vous
		asseyent	asseyent	aient	ont	aient	

†There is a variant form of the conjugation of *s'asseoir* based on the present participle *assoyant* and first person singular *assois*, but this is rather archaic and is rarely used. There are also two variant forms for the future stem: *assiér-* and *assoir-*. *Assiér-* is frequently used.

avoir to have *(avoir)*	ayant eu	ai as a avons avez ont	aie aies ait ayons ayez aient	av + ais ais ait ions iez aient	aur + ai as a ons ez ont	aur + ais ais ait ions iez aient	 aie ayons ayez
battre to beat *(avoir)*	battant battu	bats bats bat battons battez battent	batte battes batte battions battiez battent	batt + ais ais ait ions iez aient	battr + ai as a ons ez ont	battr + ais ais ait ions iez aient	 bats battons battez
boire to drink *(avoir)*	buvant bu	bois bois boit buvons buvez boivent	boive boives boive buvions buviez boivent	buv + ais ais ait ions iez aient	boir + ai as a ons ez ont	boir + ais ais ait ions iez aient	 bois buvons buvez
conclure to conclude *(avoir)*	concluant conclu	conclus conclus conclut concluons concluez concluent	conclue conclues conclue concluions concluiez concluent	conclu + ais ais ait ions iez aient	conclur + ai as a ons ez ont	conclur + ais ais ait ions iez aient	 conclus concluons concluez

Infinitive	Pres. & Past Participles	Present Indicative	Present Subjunctive	Imperfect Indicative	Future	Conditional	Imperative
conduire	conduisant	conduis	conduise	conduis + ais	conduir + ai	conduir + ais	
to drive	conduit	conduis	conduises	ais	as	ais	conduis
to lead		conduit	conduise	ait	a	ait	
(avoir)		conduisons	conduisions	ions	ons	ions	conduisons
		conduisez	conduisiez	iez	ez	iez	conduisez
		conduisent	conduisent	aient	ont	aient	
connaître	connaissant	connais	connaisse	connaiss + ais	connaîtr + ai	connaîtr + ais	
to know	connu	connais	connaisses	ais	as	ais	connais
(avoir)		connaît	connaisse	ait	a	ait	
		connaissons	connaissions	ions	ons	ions	connaissons
		connaissez	connaissiez	iez	ez	iez	connaissez
		connaissent	connaissent	aient	ont	aient	
courir	courant	cours	coure	cour + ais	courr + ai	courr + ais	
to run	couru	cours	coures	ais	as	ais	cours
(avoir)		court	coure	ait	a	ait	
		courons	courions	ions	ons	ions	courons
		courez	couriez	iez	ez	iez	courez
		courent	courent	aient	ont	aient	

<table>
<tr><td>croire
to believe
(avoir)</td><td>croyant
cru</td><td>crois
crois
croit
croyons
croyez
croient</td><td>croie
croies
croie
croyions
croyiez
croient</td><td>croy + ais
ais
ait
ions
iez
aient</td><td>croir + ai
as
a
ons
ez
ont</td><td>croir + ais
ais
ait
ions
iez
aient</td><td>crois
croyons
croyez</td></tr>
<tr><td>cueillir
to gather
to pick
(avoir)</td><td>cueillant
cueilli</td><td>cueille
cueilles
cueille
cueillons
cueillez
cueillent</td><td>cueille
cueilles
cueille
cueillions
cueilliez
cueillent</td><td>cueill + ais
ais
ait
ions
iez
aient</td><td>cueiller + ai
as
a
ons
ez
ont</td><td>cueiller + ais
ais
ait
ions
iez
aient</td><td>cueille
cueillons
cueillez</td></tr>
<tr><td>devoir
to owe
ought
(avoir)</td><td>devant
dû</td><td>dois
dois
doit
devons
devez
doivent</td><td>doive
doives
doive
devions
deviez
doivent</td><td>dev + ais
ais
ait
ions
iez
aient</td><td>devr + ai
as
a
ons
ez
ont</td><td>devr + ais
ais
ait
ions
iez
aient</td><td>not used</td></tr>
<tr><td>dire
to say
to tell
(avoir)</td><td>disant
dit</td><td>dis
dis
dit
disons
dites
disent</td><td>dise
dises
dise
disions
disiez
disent</td><td>dis + ais
ais
ait
ions
iez
aient</td><td>dir + ai
as
a
ons
ez
ont</td><td>dir + ais
ais
ait
ions
iez
aient</td><td>dis
disons
dites</td></tr>
</table>

Infinitive	Pres. & Past Participles	Present Indicative	Present Subjunctive	Imperfect Indicative	Future	Conditional	Imperative
dormir	dormant	dors	dorme	dorm + ais	dormir + ai	dormir + ais	
to sleep	dormi	dors	dormes	ais	as	ais	dors
(avoir)		dort	dorme	ait	a	ait	
		dormons	dormions	ions	ons	ions	dormons
		dormez	dormiez	iez	ez	iez	dormez
		dorment	dorment	aient	ont	aient	
écrire	écrivant	écris	écrive	écriv + ais	écrir + ai	écrir + ais	
to write	écrit	écris	écrives	ais	as	ais	écris
(avoir)		écrit	écrive	ait	a	ait	
		écrivons	écrivions	ions	ons	ions	écrivons
		écrivez	écriviez	iez	ez	iez	écrivez
		écrivent	écrivent	aient	ont	aient	
envoyer	envoyant	envoie	envoie	envoy + ais	enverr + ai	enverr + ais	
to send	envoyé	envoies	envoies	ais	as	ais	envoie
(avoir)		envoie	envoie	ait	a	ait	
		envoyons	envoyions	ions	ons	ions	envoyons
		envoyez	envoyiez	iez	ez	iez	envoyez
		envoient	envoient	aient	ont	aient	
être	étant	suis	sois	ét + ais	ser + ai	ser + ais	
to be	été	es	sois	ais	as	ais	sois
(avoir)		est	soit	ait	a	ait	
		sommes	soyons	ions	ons	ions	soyons
		étes	soyez	iez	ez	iez	soyez
		sont	soient	aient	ont	aient	

faillir† to fail *(avoir)*	faillant failli	*not used*	*not used*	*not used*	faillir + ai as a ons ez ont	faillir + ais ais ait ions iez aient	*not used*
faire to do to make *(avoir)*	faisant fait	fais fais fait faisons faites font	fasse fasses fasse fassions fassiez fassent	fais + ais ais ait ions iez aient	fer + ai as a ons ez ont	fer + ais ais ait ions iez aient	fais faisons faites
falloir to be neces-sary, must (used only with *il*) *(avoir)*	*no pres. part.* fallu	il faut	il faille	il fallait	il faudra	il faudrait	*not used*

† Used in expressions such as ***Il a failli tomber***, He nearly fell (lit., he failed to fall).

Infinitive	Pres. & Past Participles	Present Indicative	Present Subjunctive	Imperfect Indicative	Future	Conditional	Imperative
fuir	fuyant	fuis	fuie	fuy + ais	fuir + ai	fuir + ais	
to flee	fui	fuis	fuies	ais	as	ais	fuis
(avoir)		fuit	fuie	ait	a	ait	
		fuyons	fuyions	ions	ons	ions	fuyons
		fuyez	fuyiez	iez	ez	iez	fuyez
		fuient	fuient	aient	ont	aient	
haïr	haïssant	hais	haïsse	haïss + ais	haïr + ai	haïr + ais	
to hate	haï	hais	haïsses	ais	as	ais	haïs
(avoir)		hait	haïsse	ait	a	ait	
		haïssons	haïssions	ions	ions	ions	haïssons
		haïssons	haïssiez	iez	ez	iez	haïssez
		haïssent	haïssent	aient	ont	aient	
lire	lisant	lis	lise	lis + ais	lir + ai	lir + ais	
to read	lu	lis	lises	ais	as	ais	lis
(avoir)		lit	lise	ait	a	ait	
		lisons	lisions	ions	ons	ions	lisons
		lisez	lisiez	iez	ez	iez	lisez
		lisent	lisent	aient	ont	aient	

mettre to put to place *(avoir)*	mettant mis	mets mets met mettons mettez mettent	mette mettes mette mettions mettiez mettent	mett – ais ais ait ions iez aient	mettr + ai as a ons ez ont	mettr + ais ais ait ions iez aient	mets mettons mettez
mourir to die *(être)*	mourant mort(e)(s)	meurs meurs meurt mourons mourez meurent	meure meures meure mourions mouriez meurent	mour + ais ais ait ions iez aient	mourr + ai as a ons ez ont	mourr + ais ais ait ions iez aient	meurs mourons mourez
mouvoir† to move *(avoir)*	mouvant mû	meus meus meut mouvons mouvez meuvent	meuve meuves meuve mouvions mouviez meuvent	mouv + ais ais ait ions iez aient	mouvr + ai as a ons ez ont	mouvr + ais ais ait ions iez aient	meus mouvons mouvez
naître to be born *(être)*	naissant né(e)(s)	nais nais naît naissons naissez naissent	naisse naisses naisse naissions naissiez naissent	naiss – ais ais ait ions iez aient	naîtr + ai as a ons ez ont	naîtr + ais ais ait ions iez aient	nais naissons naissez

† *Mouvoir* is seldom used except in compounds like *émouvoir*, to move (emotionally).

Infinitive	Pres. & Past Participles	Present Indicative	Present Subjunctive	Imperfect Indicative	Future	Conditional	Imperative
ouvrir	ouvrant	ouvre	ouvre	ouvr + ais	ouvrir + ai	ouvrir + ais	
to open	ouvert	ouvres	ouvres	ais	as	ais	ouvre
(avoir)		ouvre	ouvre	ait	a	ait	
		ouvrons	ouvrions	ions	ons	ions	ouvrons
		ouvrez	ouvriez	iez	ez	iez	ouvrez
		ouvrent	ouvrent	aient	ont	aient	
partir	partant	pars	parte	part + ais	partir + ai	partir + ais	
to leave	parti(e)(s)	pars	partes	ais	as	ais	pars
to depart		part	parte	ait	a	ait	
(être)		partons	partions	ions	ons	ions	partons
		partez	partiez	iez	ez	iez	partez
		partent	partent	aient	ont	aient	
plaire	plaisant	plais	plaise	plais + ais	plair + ai	plair + ais	
to please	plu	plais	plaises	ais	as	ais	plais
(to be pleas-		plaît	plaise	ait	a	ait	
ing to)		plaisons	plaisions	ions	ons	ions	plaisons
(avoir)		plaisez	plaisiez	iez	ez	iez	plaisez
		plaisent	plaisent	aient	ont	aient	

pleuvoir to rain (used only with *il*) *(avoir)*	pleuvant plu	il pleut	il pleuve	il pleuvait	il pleuvra	il pleuvrait	*not used*
pouvoir† to be able, can *(avoir)*	pouvant pu	peux (puis)† peux peut pouvons pouvez peuvent	puisse puisses puisse puissons puissiez puissent	pouv + ais ais ait ions iez aient	pourr + ai as a ons ez ont	pourr + ais ais ait ions iez aient	*not used*
prendre to take *(avoir)*	prenant pris	prends prends prend prenons prenez prennent	prenne prennes prenne prenions preniez prennent	pren + ais ais ait ions iez aient	prendr + ai as a ons ez ont	prendr + ais ais ait ions iez aient	prends prenons prenez
résoudre to resolve *(avoir)*	résolvant résolu	résous résous résout résolvons résolvez résolvent	résolve résolves résolve résolvions résolviez résolvent	résolv + ais ais ait ions iez aient	résoudr + ai as a ons ez ont	résoudr + ais ais ait ions iez aient	résous résolvons résolvez

† The interrogative of *pouvoir* in the first person singular is always *Puis-je?*

Infinitive	Pres. & Past Participles	Present Indicative	Present Subjunctive	Imperfect Indicative	Future	Conditional	Imperative
rire to laugh *(avoir)*	riant ri	ris ris rit rions riez rient	rie ries rie riions riiez rient	ri + ais ais ait ions iez aient	rir + ai as a ons ez ont	rir + ais ais ait ions iez aient	 ris rions riez
savoir to know *(avoir)*	sachant su	sais sais sait savons savez savent	sache saches sache sachions sachiez sachent	sav + ais ais ait ions iez aient	saur + ai as a ons ez ont	saur + ais ais ait ions iez aient	 sache sachons sachez
suffire to be enough, to suffice *(avoir)*	suffisant suffi	suffis suffis suffit suffisons suffisez suffisent	suffise suffises suffise suffisions suffisiez suffisent	suffis + ais ais ait ions iez aient	suffir + ai as a ons ez ont	suffir + ais ais ait ions iez aient	 suffis suffisons suffisez
suivre to follow *(avoir)*	suivant suivi	suis suis suit suivons suivez suivent	suive suives suive suivions suiviez suivent	suiv + ais ais ait ions iez aient	suivr + ai as a ons ez ont	suivr + ais ais ait ions iez aient	 suis suivons suivez

(se)taire to be quiet to say nothing *(être)*	taisant tu(e)(s)	tais tais tait taisons taisez taisent	taise taises taise taisions taisiez taisent	tais + ais ais ait ions iez aient	tair + ai as a ons ez ont	tair + ais ais ait ions iez aient	 tais-toi taisons-nous taisez-vous
tenir to hold to keep *(avoir)*	tenant tenu	tiens tiens tient tenons tenez tiennent	tienne tiennes tienne tenions teniez tiennent	ten + ais ais ait ions iez aient	tiendr + ai as a ons ez ont	tiendr + ais ais ait ions iez aient	 tiens tenons tenez
vaincre to conquer *(avoir)*	vainquant vaincu	vaincs vaincs vainc vainquons vainquez vainquent	vainque vainques vainque vainquions vainquiez vainquent	vainqu + ais ais ait ions iez aient	vaincr + ai as a ons ez ont	vaincr + ais ais ait ions iez aient	 vaincs vainquons vainquez
valoir to be worth *(avoir)*	valant valu	vaux vaux vaut valons valez valent	vaille vailles vaille valions valiez vaillent	val + ais ais ait ions iez aient	vaudr + ai as a ons ez ont	vaudr + ais ais ait ions iez aient	 vaux † valons valez

†The imperative of *valoir* is not often used.

venir to come *(être)*	venant venu(e)(s)	viens viens vient venons venez viennent	vienne viennes vienne venions veniez viennent	ven + ais ais ait ions iez aient	viendr + ai as a ons ez ont	viendr + ais ais ait ions iez aient	 viens venons venez
vivre to live *(avoir)*	vivant vécu	vis vis vit vivons vivez vivent	vive vives vive vivions viviez vivent	viv + ais ais ait ions iez aient	vivr + ai as a ons ez ont	vivr + ais ais ait ions iez aient	 vis vivons vivez
voir to see *(avoir)*	voyant vu	vois vois voit voyons voyez voient	voie voies voie voyions voyiez voient	voy + ais ais ait ions iez aient	verr + ai as a ons ez ont	verr + ais ais ait ions iez aient	 vois voyons voyez
vouloir to wish to want *(avoir)*	voulant voulu	veux veux veut voulons voulez veulent	veuille veuilles veuille voulions vouliez veuillent	voul + ais ais ait ions iez aient	voudr + ai as a ons ez ont	voudr + ais ais ait ions iez aient	 veuillez†

† This is the only form of the imperative of *vouloir* generally used.

LETTER WRITING

LETTER WRITING

1. FORMAL INVITATIONS AND ACCEPTANCES

FORMAL INVITATIONS

Monsieur et madame de Montour vous prient de leur faire l'honneur d'assister à un bal, donné en l'honneur de leur fille Marie-José, le dimanche huit avril à neuf heures du soir.

M. et Mme. de Montour
35 Avenue Hoche
Paris xvi ème.

R.S.V.P.

Mr. and Mrs. de Montour request the pleasure of your presence at a ball given in honor of their daughter, Marie-José, on Sunday evening, April the eighth, at nine o'clock.

Mr. and Mrs. de Montour
35 avenue Hoche
Paris xvi ème.

R.S.V.P.

R.S.V.P. stands for *Répondez s'il vous plaît.* Please answer.

NOTE OF ACCEPTANCE

Monsieur et madame du Panier vous remercient de votre aimable invitation à laquelle ils se feront un plaisir de se rendre.

Mr. and Mrs. du Panier thank you for your kind invitation and will be delighted to come.

2. THANK-YOU NOTES

le 14 mars 1956

Chère Madame,

Je tiens à vous remercier de l'aimable attention que vous avez eue en m'envoyant le charmant présent que j'ai reçu. Ce tableau me fait d'autant plus plaisir qu'il est ravissant dans le cadre de mon studio.

Je vous prie de croire à l'expression de mes sentiments de sincère amitié.

Renée Beaujoly

March 14, 1956

Dear Mrs. Duparc,

I should like to thank you for the delightful present you sent me. The picture was all the more welcome because it fits in so beautifully with the other things in my studio.

Thank you ever so much.

Sincerely yours,
Renée Beaujoly

3. BUSINESS LETTERS

M. Roger Beaumont
2 rue Chalgrin
Paris

le 6 novembre 1955
M. le rédacteur en chef
"Vu"
3 Blvd. des Capucines
Paris

Monsieur,

Je vous envoie ci-inclus mon chèque de 120 frs., montant de ma souscription d'un abonnement d'un an à votre publication.

Veuillez agréer, Monsieur, mes salutations distinguées.

Roger Beaumont

ci-inclus un chèque

2 Chalgrin Street
Paris
November 6th, 1955

Circulation Department
"Vu"
3 Blvd. des Capucines
Paris

Gentlemen:

Inclosed please find a check for 120 francs to cover a year's subscription to your magazine.

Sincerely yours,
Roger Beaumont

Inc.

Dupuis Aîné
3 rue du Quatre-Septembre
Paris.

le 30 septembre 1955
Vermont et Cie.
2 rue Marat
Bordeaux
Gironde

Monsieur,

En réponse à votre lettre du dix courant, je tiens à vous confirmer que la marchandise en question vous a été expédiée le treize août par colis postal.

Veuillez agréer, Monsieur, mes salutations distinguées,

Henri Tournaire

db/ht

3 Quatre-Septembre St.
Paris
September 30, 1955

Vermont and Co.
2 Marat Street
Bordeaux
Gironde

Gentlemen:

In reply to your letter of the 10th of this month, I wish to confirm that the merchandise was mailed to you parcel post on August the 13th.

Sincerely yours,

Henri Tournaire

db/ht

4. INFORMAL LETTERS

le 5 mars 1955

Mon cher Jacques,

Ta derniere lettre m'a fait grand plaisir.

Tout d'abord laisse-moi t'annoncer une bonne nouvelle: je compte venir passer une quinzaine de jours à Paris au commencement d'avril et je me réjouis à l'avance à l'idée de te revoir ainsi que les tiens qui je l'espère, se portent bien.

Colette vient avec moi et se fait une grande joie à l'idée de connaître enfin ta femme, de cette manière nous pourrons laisser nos deux femmes potiner un après-midi et nous pourrons rester ensemble comme nous faisions au lycée. Les affaires marchent bien en ce moment, espérons que ça continuera. Tâche de ne pas avoir trop de malades au mois d'avril, enfin il est vrai que ces choses-là ne se commandent pas.

Toute ma famille se porte bien, heureusement.

J'ai pris l'apéritif avec Dumont l'autre jour, qui m'a demandé de tes nouvelles. Son affaire marche très bien.

J'allais presque oublier le plus important, peux-tu me réserver une chambre au Grand Hôtel pour le cinq avril, je t'en saurais fort gré.

J'espère avoir le plaisir de te lire très bientôt.

Mes respects à ta femme et pour toi une amicale poignée de main,

ton ami,
André

March 5th, 1955

Dear Jack,

I was very happy to receive your last letter.

First of all, I've some good news for you. I expect to spend two weeks in Paris at the beginning of April and I'm looking forward to the prospect of seeing you and your family, all of whom I hope are well.

Colette's coming with me; she's delighted to be able at last to meet your wife. That way we shall be able to let our two wives gossip and we can spend the afternoon talking together as we used to at school. Business is pretty good right now. Let's hope it will keep up. Try not to get too many patients during the month of April, though I suppose that's a little difficult to arrange.

I had cocktails with Dumont the other day and he asked about you. His business is going well.

I almost forgot the most important thing. Can you reserve a room for me at the Grand Hotel for April the fifth? You'll be doing me a great favor.

I hope to hear from you soon. My best regards to your wife.

Yours,
Andrew

Paris, le 3 avril 1955

Ma Chérie,

J'ai bien reçu ta lettre du trente et je suis heureuse de savoir que ta fille est tout à fait remise.

Rien de bien nouveau ici, sauf que Pierre me donne beaucoup de mal, enfin toi aussi tu as un fils de cet âge-là, et tu sais ce que je veux dire!

L'autre jour, j'ai rencontré Mme Michaud dans la rue, Dieu qu'elle a vieilli! Elle est méconnaissable!

Ma femme de chambre vient de me quitter, les domestiques deviennent insupportables à Paris, tu as bien de la veine d'être à la montagne pour encore un mois.

Nous avons vu ton mari l'autre soir, il est venu dîner à la maison; il se porte bien et voudrait bien te voir de retour.

Que fais-tu de beau toute la journée à Chamonix? Y-a-t-il encore beaucoup de monde là-bas? Il paraît que les de Villneque sont là. A Paris tout le monde parle des prochaines fiançailles de leur fille.

Nous sommes allés à une soirée l'autre soir chez les Clergeaud, cette femme ne sait pas recevoir, je m'y suis ennuyée à mourir.

Voilà à peu près tous les derniers potins de Paris, tu vois que je te tiens bien au courant, tâche d'en faire autant.

Embrasse bien Françoise pour moi.

Meilleurs baisers de ton amie,
Monique

Paris, April 3rd, 1955

Darling,

I received your letter of the 30th and I'm happy to learn that your daughter has completely recovered.

Nothing new here, except that Peter is giving me a lot of trouble. You have a son of the same age, so you know what I mean.

The other day I ran into Mrs. Michaud in the street. My, how she's aged! She's unrecognizable!

My chambermaid just left me; servants in Paris are becoming impossible. You're lucky to be staying in the mountains for another month.

We saw your husband the other night—he had dinner at our house. He's well and is looking forward to your coming home.

What do you do all day long in Chamonix? Is it still very crowded? It seems that the de Villneques are there. In Paris, the future engagement of their daughter is the talk of the town.

The other evening we went to a dull party given by the Clergeauds. She doesn't know how to entertain and I was bored to death.

That's about all of the latest Paris gossip. You see how well I keep you posted- try to do the same.

Give my love to Frances.

Love,

Monique

5. FORMS OF SALUTATIONS AND COMPLIMENTARY CLOSINGS

SALUTATIONS

Formal

Monsieur l'Abbé,	Dear Reverend:
Monsieur le Député,	Dear Congressman:
Monsieur le Maire,	Dear Mayor (Smith):
Cher Professeur,	Dear Professor (Smith):
Cher Maître, (Mon cher Maître,)	Dear Mr. (Smith): (Lawyers are addressed as "Maître" in France.)
Monsieur,	Dear Sir:
Messieurs,	Gentlemen:
Cher Monsieur Varnoux,	My dear Mr. Varnoux:
Chère Madame Gignoux,	My dear Mrs. Gignoux:

Informal

Mon Cher Roger,	Dear Roger,
Ma Chère Denise,	Dear Denise,
Chéri,	Darling (*m.*),
Chérie,	Darling (*f.*),
Mon Chéri,	My darling (*m.*),
Ma Chérie,	My darling (*f.*),

Formal

1. *Agréez, je vous prie, l'expression de mes salutations les plus distinguées.*
   ("Please accept the expression of my most distinguished greetings.") Very truly yours.
2. *Veuillez agréer l'expression de mes salutations distinguées.*
   ("Will you please accept the expression of my distinguished greetings.") Very truly yours.
3. *Veuillez agréer, Monsieur, mes salutations empressées.*
   ("Sir, please accept my eager greetings.") Yours truly.
4. *Veuillez agréer, Monsieur, mes sincères salutations.*
   ("Sir, please accept my sincere greetings.") Yours truly.
5. *Agréez, Monsieur, mes salutations distinguées.*
   ("Sir, accept my distinguished greetings.") Yours truly.
6. *Votre tout dévoué.*
   ("Your very devoted.") Yours truly.

Informal

1. *Je vous prie de croire à l'expression de mes sentiments de sincère amitié.*
   ("Please believe in my feelings of sincere friendship.") Very sincerely.
2. *Meilleures amitiés.*
   ("Best friendship.") Sincerely yours.
3. *Amicalement.*
   ("Kindly.") Sincerely yours.
4. *Mes pensées affectueuses* (or *amicales*).
   ("My affectionate *or* friendly thoughts.") Sincerely.
5. *Une poignée de main amicale.*
   ("A friendly handshake.") Sincerely.
6. *Je te serre la main.*
   ("I shake your hand.") Sincerely.

7. *Affectueusement.*
   Affectionately.
8. *Très affectueusement.*
   ("Very affectionately.") Affectionately yours.
9. *Je vous prie de bien vouloir transmettre mes respects à Madame votre mère.*
   Please give my regards to your mother.
10. *Transmets mes respects à ta famille.*
    Give my regards to your family.
11. *Rappelle-moi au bon souvenir de ta famille.*
    Remember me to your family.
12. *Embrasse tout le monde pour moi.*
    ("Kiss everybody for me.") Give my love to everybody.
13. *Je t'embrasse bien fort.*
    Millions de baisers. } Love.

6. FORM OF THE ENVELOPE

Vermont et Cie.
5 rue Daunou
Paris 2 ème

Maison Dupuis Aîné
2 cours de l'Intendance
Bordeaux, Gironde

M. Jean Alexandre
6 rue Marat
Grenoble
Isère

M. Robert Marcatour
aux bons soins[1] de M.P. Lambert
2 rue du Ranelagh
Paris xvi ème

---

[1] "In care of." Sometimes written as in English: C/o.